How to Create a
Culture of **Achievement**

in your school and classroom

ASCD MEMBER BOOK

Many ASCD members received this book as a
member benefit upon its initial release.

Learn more at: **www.ascd.org/memberbooks**

How to Create a Culture of
Achievement

in your school and classroom

Douglas **Fisher** • Nancy **Frey** • Ian **Pumpian**

 | Alexandria, Virginia

ASCD®

1703 N. Beauregard St. • Alexandria, VA 22311-1714 USA
Phone: 800-933-2723 or 703-578-9600 • Fax: 703-575-5400
Website: www.ascd.org • E-mail: member@ascd.org
Author guidelines: www.ascd.org/write

Gene R. Carter, *Executive Director;* Ed Milliken, *Chief Program Development Officer;* Carole Hayward, *Publisher;* Julie Houtz, *Director, Book Editing & Production;* Deborah Siegel, *Editor;* Sima Nasr, *Senior Graphic Designer;* Mike Kalyan, *Production Manager;* Valerie Younkin, *Desktop Publishing Specialist;* Kyle Steichen, *Production Specialist*

Printed in the United States of America. Cover art © 2012 by ASCD. ASCD publications present a variety of viewpoints. The views expressed or implied in this book should not be interpreted as official positions of the Association.

All web links in this book are correct as of the publication date below but may have become inactive or otherwise modified since that time. If you notice a deactivated or changed link, please e-mail books@ascd.org with the words "Link Update" in the subject line. In your message, please specify the web link, the book title, and the page number on which the link appears.

ASCD Member Book, No. FY12-7 (May 2012, P). ASCD Member Books mail to Premium (P), Select (S), and Institutional Plus (I+) members on this schedule: Jan., PSI+; Feb., P; Apr., PSI+; May, P; July, PSI+; Aug., P; Sept., PSI+; Nov., PSI+; Dec., P. Select membership was formerly known as Comprehensive membership.

PAPERBACK ISBN: **978-1-4166-1408-1**   ASCD product **#111014**

Also available as an e-book (see Books in Print for the ISBNs).

Quantity discounts for the paperback edition only: 10–49 copies, 10%; 50+ copies, 15%; for 1,000 or more copies, call 800-933-2723, ext. 5634, or 703-575-5634. For desk copies: member@ascd.org.

Library of Congress Cataloging-in-Publication Data
Fisher, Douglas, 1965-
  How to create a culture of achievement in your school and classroom / Douglas Fisher, Nancy Frey, Ian Pumpian.
    p. cm.
  Includes bibliographical references and index.
  ISBN 978-1-4166-1408-1 (pbk. : alk. paper)
1. School improvement programs—United States. 2. Academic achievement—United States. 3. School management and organization—United States. 4. School environment—United States. I. Frey, Nancy, 1959- II. Pumpian, Ian. III. Title.
  LB2822.82.F57 2012
  371.2′07—dc23
                                                                2012000762

22 21 20 19 18 17 16 15 14 13 12 11   1 2 3 4 5 6 7 8 9 10 11 12

How to Create a Culture of **Achievement**

in your school and classroom

Introduction

The part of a tree that we can readily see is above the surface. But because we understand that this living organism needs to sustain itself, we realize that there is just as much happening below. And we know that damaging its roots or poisoning its soil can result in the death of the tree.

A school's culture works in much the same way. There are things we can readily see; these are the procedures of the school. But we know that there are other elements below the surface, which serve to nurture the whole. These are our ways of work, and they speak to the relationships between and among people, as well as the ways we choose to inform ourselves. Margaret Wheatley (1998) describes the three elements that lie above the surface of an organization as its processes, structures, and patterns. We add tools to this list, as these are the ways an organization measures itself. All of these are easily seen and typically what people will first invoke when discussing a school's culture. But the underlying elements, those that are not readily observed, are equally essential, and include the relationships, identity, and connections (Wheatley, 1998). We add data to this list. These factors exist whether we choose to examine them or not. And as with any living organism, what happens both above the ground and below it needs to be cared for to sustain the school's culture.

The mission of the school should capture all of these elements, surface them, and integrate them. The mission is the starting point, not the ending point. Everyone involved in the school—from parents and students, to teachers, staff, and administrators, to external auditors and community members—needs to know the mission and how their work supports it. From the mission, schools and their leaders need a specified set of purposeful language, actions, and routines designed to make students and other stakeholders feel welcome, comfortable, important, and understood. They also need a specified set of purposeful language, actions, and routines that identify organizational systems—practices that build the culture of achievement. That's what this book is about: creating and implementing a system to operationalize the mission and, in doing so, ensure that students achieve.

Organizational Practices That Build Culture

This book will offer some suggested practices and structures to help schools get into a cycle of continuous improvement driven by mission, inspired by vision, and operationalized by culture. The practices are organized by *pillars*, or overarching ideas that communicate to stakeholders how the school's mission will be kept alive to thrive in the daily life of the school. We selected the term "pillar" because it is an architectural element that is designed to transmit weight within a structure. In other words, the pillars hold things up. Pillars are the structures that hold up the mission statement. They are the link between the mission statement and the ground on which people teach and learn.

Over the past several years, our collective experience in schools and our wide reading of business and education books have led us to identify five pillars that are critical to the culture of achievement that each of us hopes to build. These five pillars, each with a chapter devoted to explaining it, are as follows:

1. Welcome
2. Do no harm
3. Choice words
4. It's never too late to learn
5. Best school in the universe

In chapters 2 through 6, each pillar is explained. We discuss why that pillar is important in building culture, and we provide examples from schools as the staff within the building has worked to implement that pillar. In addition, each chapter highlights practices and structures to ensure that the pillar becomes part of the daily practices within the school. These features include the following:

1. **Organizational principles,** the specific components of the pillar that provide definitions and examples of quality implementation.
2. **Service cycles,** a series of actions that staff understand are essential to operationalizing the school's mission and its pillars.
3. **Action research tools,** a means to balance and align investment in reflective practice, responsive planning, and competent performance.

By examining what lies above the surface of a school's organization, we can expose what lies below—the relationships, identity, culture, and data that are necessary to anchor and sustain the school. The image can be found in figure i.1.

The collective power of a school community that turns its attention to building a culture of achievement cannot be underestimated. As with trees to be nurtured, the care and maintenance of our resources provides us with the shade we need.

FIGURE i.1

Above and Below the Organizational Surface

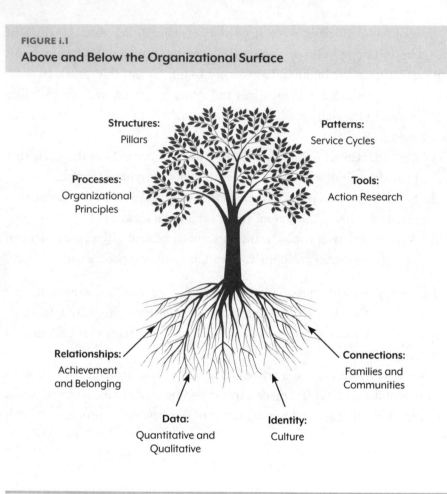

CHAPTER 1

Creating Culture in Schools

An underground flow of feelings and folkways [wending] its way within schools in the form of vision and values, beliefs and assumptions, rituals and ceremonies, history and stories, and physical symbols. (Deal & Peterson, 1999, pp. 7–8)

This book proposes that effective organizations, including schools, should make building culture part of a planned strategic effort. Most school improvement plans concentrate on academic achievement goals, decisions about academic focus, deployment of instructional models, and teaching techniques and curriculum tools. Most school improvement plans therefore aspire to create academic focus, an academic sense of responsibility, intensity, and urgency—that is, an "academic press" (Lee & Smith, 1999). Academic press is absolutely necessary, but not sufficient to operationalize the mission of the school. We believe that no school improvement effort will be effective, maintained, or enhanced unless school culture and academic press are both addressed and aligned. Both developing school culture and creating academic press are necessary, but neither is in and of itself sufficient.

We suggest that these two elements of school effectiveness must be integrated and unified. Heretofore, researchers have referred to two curricula operating in the school. The first is the academic curriculum, which has been described as the objective, explicit curriculum of the school. The second is school culture—the implicit curriculum of the school. In this book, we propose that a school's culture should not be underground and assumed. It should be uncovered, openly and purposely discussed, assessed, and developed. School culture cannot be hidden and implicit; rather, it must be as explicit as our approach to teaching and learning. In fact, we propose that our academic press and our school culture should be looked at, thought about, and acted upon in a unified and coordinated manner.

Cultures are not created overnight or by pen and planning alone. Jerald (2006) argues that culture is born from an organization's vision, beliefs, values, and mission. Stating your mission is significant, but only a small part of your effort. Culture develops and grows up through an accumulation of *actions, traditions, symbols, ceremonies, and rituals that are closely aligned with that vision.*

According to Deal and Peterson (2009), research suggests that a strong, positive culture serves several beneficial functions, including the following:
- Fostering effort and productivity.
- Improving collegial and collaborative activities that in turn promote better communication and problem solving.
- Supporting successful change and improvement efforts.
- Building commitment and helping students and teachers identify with the school.
- Amplifying energy and motivation of staff members and students.
- Focusing attention and daily behavior on what is important and valued.

So we have purposely worked at developing school culture in ways that will further engage each student in a world-class educational experience. The looking, thinking, and acting we will encourage will be about increasing a culture of educational engagement by promoting
1. A culture that is *welcoming,*
2. A culture in which the *conditions for learning are ever-present,*
3. A culture in which we examine *how our behaviors affect us, others, and our world,*
4. A culture in which there is a shared belief that we are a *part of something special and great,* and

5. A culture in which the language creates and facilitates *personal pride, purpose and power.*

Cultures: Yes, Schools and Students Have Them

We believe that culture must be purposely developed and managed to optimize the chance to live our mission, become our vision, and fulfill our educational purpose and responsibilities. We also recognize that our students bring their cultures with them. Consider the following students, all enrolling in a local high school.

Amal is a 14-year-old girl. For the past six years she has attended an Islamic private school. Prior to that she was homeschooled. To this point in her life she has had virtually no unsupervised interactions with males outside her immediate family. She has a strong fundamental cultural identity as a Muslim girl.

Renee is also 14 years old. She has been homeschooled all her life. Her family organized the homeschooling of their children with other members of their church. Renee has a strong sense of culture from the values instilled in her by her family and her Christian faith.

Eddie chose this school to provide some separation between his schooling and his friends who are involved in gangs and attend what would have been Eddie's school. Despite his school choice, gang involvement is a large part of his family, his extended family, his current friends, and his community. That culture is a part of who Eddie presently is. Life on the streets dictates certain rules of survival, such as "fight back and defend family" and "retaliate when you or your family is disrespected."

Stephen chose to enroll in the school because of its unique health science career focus with industry-based internships. Stephen has always expected to attend college and graduate school and become a doctor. He gave up the opportunity to attend a high-performing suburban high school to attend one that catered to his niche interests. Stephen comes to school with a lot of cultural capital that has always made him a driven and successful student.

Tony attends the school because of the influence that a community mentor has had on his life for many years. Tony lives with his mother, his four siblings, and extended family members who have come and gone over the years. His mother's health limits her activity outside the home, and the family depends on public assistance. Tony has never been particularly interested or successful in school. His propensity to sleep in and ignore his alarm is frequent, as is his absenteeism. Tony expresses no postschool plans, and his commitment to graduate is weak. Tony's behavior is shaped by the challenges of living in a sphere of generational poverty.

These real vignettes are wrought with biting and predictable stereotypes. We assure you that each of these young people is a unique individual packed with obvious and hidden attributes, interests, talents, and gifts. Each has aspirations and nightmares that are influenced by every opportunity given to them and by every opportunity they were denied. The fact remains, however, that each of these unique individuals will come to school with a cultural identity that is based on his or her experiences. That culture has provided much of the context for how these individuals view the world.

So this book is also about the culture of schools populated by individuals. Although others may suggest that conscious attention to creating school culture may be mostly to promote student achievement, especially when the school population is diverse and includes many who may not have had experiences developing the cultural capital leading to successful public school performance, the five new students we profiled taught us otherwise. As a public school, we should at least expect that the school culture will be more pluralistic than many of these students have experienced. It may be less tolerant of behaviors they know that help them survive on the streets. It will certainly be committed to graduation and postsecondary planning. The public school will be more tolerant of differing views about sex, religion, politics, and discipline than some students have been raised to believe, while others may see the school's view as narrow and restricting. The fact is that students enter the culture of the school with an intact cultural identity that has been formed from already being part of one or more home and community cultures. The job of school, then, is to foster a bicultural student body—one that recognizes the home culture while creating a school one.

A diverse student body also means that students who have many different cultural histories are about to converge on a setting that hosts them all. On that point, *know now that we believe that teaching tolerance, understanding, and respect is a nonnegotiable part of creating an effective school culture.* We believe that creating an effective school culture for a student who arrives with a dissimilar cultural identity and history is likely to make a student bicultural. An effective school culture will provide students a respectful mediating experience through which they can understand, examine, affirm, modify, or change understandings of the world and how they want to engage in it. The bicultural experience will be pluralistic to the extent that each student will feel respected, welcomed, and included within that which defines the school. What is the alternative to a bicultural experience? If left to chance, if students feel prejudged and unwanted, they will create cultural cliques and take separate and parallel journeys through the school. They will not belong, feel ownership, and engage in the school or its mission. Their perspective of the school culture will be that there is no place for them, and that the school is not a place they want to be part of or a place where they choose to engage.

The other extreme to bicultural identity may be a wholesale rejection of all they believe and all the values and beliefs they have come to school with. If this means a rejection of behaviors and rituals that are illegal, undeniably destructive and antisocial, all the better. But public schools cannot be in the business of purposefully changing Republicans into Democrats or making pro-choice activists out of right-to-life believers (or vice versa). Public schools should be about creating understanding and tolerance regardless of students' personal moral and religious beliefs; and if information, reflection, and maturity solidifies their choices, causes them to doubt their choices, or changes their choices, so be it. The fact is Amal, Renee, Eddie, Stephen, and Tony have cultural identities and histories. School should provide them the safe opportunity to share their narrative, to tell their story, and to start writing the next several chapters of the person whom they aspire to be.

The Culture Must Facilitate Quality

As we have noted, having a mission is an important first step in improving student achievement, because it focuses the various people inside the organization on a common purpose. We are reminded of a school that had four different major educational reform efforts as their focus. Different teachers concentrated on different reforms. The reform efforts were not bad ideas—in fact some of them were really good. But the fact that different people were focused on different things made it hard for them to reach agreements and then focus on quality implementation of the ideas. When there is agreement on the focus, work gets directed toward that focus. We know of an elementary school, for example, that focused on writing instruction. Their mission included attention to students' communication skills, and the members of this school community agreed that writing was a need. As they honed their skills, they increased their understanding of quality instruction and were able to have some excellent conversations with one another about what worked and what did not.

Lasting change requires an agreement on quality such that the leader and the teacher can have a productive conversation. We'll come back to this point later, but our experiences with school improvement efforts suggest that reaching agreements on quality are crucial if professional development efforts and administrative or peer feedback are going to be effective.

As an example, think back to a conversation you've had with a teacher following a classroom observation. Say, for example, that you just returned from a conference that validated and extended your understanding of the importance of building on students' background knowledge. As part of the observation, you notice several opportunities that the teacher missed to build and activate background knowledge. The conversation you have with the teacher might go something like this:

Leader: How do you think the lesson went?

Teacher: Great, I thought that my students were all engaged.

Leader: Yes, true, they all seemed interested in the topic. Did you think about what they might already know about the topic? Or what they might not know about the topic?

Teacher: No, not really. I think that they learned a lot from the experience. Did you hear them talking with each other?

Leader: Yes, they were talking and asking good questions. But what did they already know?

Teacher: I'm not sure. But I will bet that they do well on the assessment.

Leader: Did you think about making connections between their background knowledge and the topic at hand? Could it be that some of the students already knew this before the lesson?

Teacher: Sure, but that's what happens in every lesson. Some know it already, some get it, and others need more teaching.

Leader: I think it would be useful to tap into students' background knowledge and then build on that with students.

Teacher: Yeah, maybe. I really liked the summaries they wrote at the end. You didn't get to see that part, but I can show you what they wrote. See...

This conversation isn't really getting anywhere, because the two people have a different understanding of quality, at least in terms of the topic of background knowledge. As a result, the teacher is immune to the feedback being provided and is not likely to change as a result of the experience.

As Goetsch and Davis (2010) note, people often define quality using specifications, standards, and other measures. It is useful for organizations to pay attention to the ways that their customers define quality. In different segments of the economy, people deal with quality differently. No matter what sector of the economy people are in, quality always affects their daily routines and lives. People are concerned with quality when grocery shopping, eating in a restaurant, and when making a purchasing decision. The definition of quality is the standard of something as measured against other things of a similar kind.

Having a shared definition of quality is important because it becomes part of the culture. A shared definition of quality also enlists all members of the culture, not just a few, to take an active part in the effort. Importantly, it also empowers people by sending them the message that they are of value and their contributions are essential. As educational leadership researcher and expert Michael Fullan notes: "Deep and sustained reform depends on many of us, not just on the few who are destined to be extraordinary" (2001, p. 2). Culture is built through shared experiences and language. Structuring the culture of a school such that quality is the focus leads to increased achievement. To do this, we draw on proven organizational responses to create that structure.

Proven Organizational Responses

In this book, we suggest a set of structures that we believe are needed to align actions and performance with the mission. Many of these structures are drawn from a variety of provocative and proven educational and business leaders. These include the works of bestselling authors, reports from recognized researchers, and analyses of highly successful organizations. Of note are structures we draw from Malcolm Baldrige National Quality Award–winning organizations. According to their website (http://www.nist.gov/baldrige/about/index.cfm), Baldrige is federally funded and organized by the National Institute of Standards and Technology. The Baldrige group is "the nation's public-private partnership dedicated to performance excellence." Baldrige recognizes organizations in different sectors, including education, health care, manufacturing, nonprofit/government, service, and small business. For the education sector, there are seven areas of concentration:

1. Leadership
2. Strategic Planning
3. Customer Focus
4. Measurement, Analysis, and Knowledge Management
5. Workforce Focus
6. Operations Focus
7. Results

It is worth noting that the education sector of Baldrige includes a focus on the customer. While this term is most often used in business communities, the Baldrige team understands that there are a number of different customers in a school learning community. Obviously, this includes the student. But it should also include family members, teachers, staff, administrators, and community members. The culture of the school has to serve all of the customers well, not just one group.

One of our doctoral students, Cindy Lewis, who works for the San Diego Municipal Airport and is responsible for professional development, devoted her dissertation to the study of Baldrige award–winning organizations. She examined five different winners from five different sectors. She found that these diverse organizations shared a number of common practices in their quest for excellence. We contend that these organizations purposefully developed strategic plans to operationalize the organizations they wanted to emmulate. They used a series of structures to bring their mission to life. These organizations did not leave the development of their culture to chance. And we believe effective schools can do no less.

Action Research

We respond to the need for a balanced investment in thoughtful reflection, planning, and implementation using Stringer's (2007) action research process. His "look, think, act, and look again" design provides for a dynamic cycle of ongoing and continuous improvement. It provides a cycle in which action is the expected response to thoughtful reflection and responsive planning. If mission building and revisiting is designed as a pivotal and integral driver of a school's ongoing implementation revolution, it is unlikely that the mission will be treated as something you did two years ago in a hotel meeting room. Instead teachers, parents, students, and community partners will know your mission, see your vision, and better understand your actions, interactions, investments, and decisions.

As Stringer noted in his community development work with Aboriginal people, action research encourages practitioners to collect information, analyze that information, make decisions, and then begin the process again. Stringer's work also emphasizes the various ways in which data can be collected and serves as a reminder not to limit information sources to norm-referenced student performance. Although action research can be conducted by individuals, the cycle of continually examining data and making decisions is also consistent with the idea that groups can consider larger data sets and make bigger changes in their school and its culture (Calhoun, 1999).

In each chapter of this book, we provide tools that can be used in the action research cycle. There are more tools than you will probably use in a given school year. You will want to choose the tools you use based on the actions that need to be taken. These tools can be found in the appendix of the book. For example, the Baldrige group provides a self-analysis tool that provides an opportunity for teams to reflect on their key strengths and key opportunities for improvement in each of the seven areas. This tool can be found in the appendix—action research tool 1.

In addition, action research tool 2 provides guidance on the development of a mission statement. It is important that the work done to build the culture of achievement be centered on a mission. We agree with Chris Bart, professor of strategic market leadership at McMaster University in Hamilton, Canada, who suggested, "Mission Statements can be one of the most despised management tools if implemented ineffectively" (http://www.brs-inc.com/news002.html). Our job as educational leaders is to implement mission statements wisely. This requires that people understand the mission and that there are procedures and practices put into place such that the mission drives the work that people do every day.

Finally, in action research tool 3, we recommend that you begin a SWOT analysis (SWOT stands for strengths, weaknesses, opportunities, and threats). This chart will likely be updated as you engage with the contents of this book and the school community in which you work, but it is important to begin the process of understanding that every organization has strengths, weaknesses, opportunities, and threats. The SWOT analysis will guide many actions and reactions you have over the course of creating a positive school culture. We have found it helpful to talk with people about each of these areas and assemble information as you collect it. Doing so paints an interesting picture of the school. We also suggest keeping this tool handy so that it can be updated as appropriate and shared with others who want to know more about the school. We will return to the SWOT analysis in the final chapter of this book.

Organizational Principles Related to School Culture

In each chapter, we present a number of organizational principles based on the topic of the chapter. We think of these as "must haves" to fully implement and operationalize the content from the chapter. For this chapter, the principles we have addressed include the following:

1. A mission and vision developed or revisited by a representative group of current stakeholders.

2. A specified set of purposeful language, actions, and routines designed to make students and other stakeholders feel welcome, comfortable, important, and understood.

3. A specified set of purposeful language, actions, and routines designed to help students and other stakeholders identify the expectations of each pillar.

4. A focus on quality, including quality instruction, quality interactions, and a cycle of continuous, quality improvement.

5. Continual attention to creating a passionate and competent staff capable of implementing culture-building systems.

Conclusion

An effective school operationalizes its mission by integrating academic press as part of building a positive culture. School culture is an important part of the work that educators need to do if students are going to achieve at high levels. As has been noted before, teachers matter, and what they do matters most. Yes, teachers need to have instructional skills and an understanding of their content area. But we argue that there is something else needed, and that is the systematic implementation of procedures that build the culture of the school such that students, and every other stakeholder in the educational organization, become bicultural. The culture of the school is not something that can be left to chance, nor can it be seen as something beyond our control. We have a duty to build a positive, responsive, and dynamic culture. In doing so, we can help all students, including Amal, Renee, Eddie, Stephen, and Antonio.

CHAPTER 2

Welcome

Nancy supervises student teachers, which allows her to form a lot of first impressions of schools. One assignment was at a school she had never been to before. After making a few wrong turns, she finally arrived at the school but was a bit flustered about getting there so close to the scheduled time. Although the front office was empty, the person at the front counter didn't bother to look up. After her greeting was ignored, Nancy stood by while she waited for the woman to finish with her papers. A few uncomfortable minutes later, the woman glanced up and said, "You need something?" Nancy explained who she was and began to hand the woman her university identification card, but the woman dismissed it with a wave her hand and motioned to a binder at the other end of the counter. "Visitors sign in over there."

The binder was a revelation. Although enrollment at this school was nearly 500, the list of visitors was sparse. Despite the fact that it was nearly lunchtime, Nancy was the first visitor that day. After signing in, she told the woman the classroom number and asked where it was located.

"Go out the door and make a right," the woman said, never looking up from her desk. "You'll see it." Nancy left the interaction feeling the grim atmosphere of a school that had adopted a bunker mentality.

Coincidentally, later that afternoon Nancy was a participant at an educational leadership summit being held at the local Ritz-Carlton hotel. Although she got lost again (she is directionality challenged), she drove up a few minutes before the meeting was to begin. She was greeted by a smiling valet who introduced himself, asked her name, and inquired about her travels. She left her car with him and walked into the hotel, surprised that others greeted her by name. She was not aware of the system that the hotel uses to pass along information that further personalizes one's arrival. When she asked about the meeting location, she was escorted there by an employee. Every staff member whom she saw looked her in the eye and greeted her as they passed. She felt utterly and completely *welcome*. The stress of her travels was gone. Within the first few moments of arriving she knew she was going to have an amazing experience.

The *Welcome* Pillar

Here are the essential questions related to this pillar: Can our school be so welcoming, so inviting, and so comfortable that every person who walks through our doors believes they are about to have an amazing experience? Quite simply, can our stakeholders (that is, our visitors, vendors, parents, staff, and students) feel *welcomed*?

There must be one simple answer to these questions, and that is an emphatic yes! If we do not believe it is possible to create a welcoming environment, then we really have to reexamine what we expect from our stakeholders. If they do not feel *welcome*, how can we expect them to participate, engage, and achieve? What we do know is that stakeholders develop an allegiance based on the experiences they have with the organization. Just think about Nancy's experience as a visitor to the Ritz for a conference; some day she might choose to be a return customer because she had felt welcomed and respected. She mattered. The experience is what will draw her back. Organizational theorists have a term for this: the experience economy.

The Experience Economy

Harvard's Joe Pine and James Gilmore (2011) theorized that the current economy is based on experience, whereas previous economies were built around agriculture, industry, or service. To be successful today, organizations must create memorable experiences for their customers, and the memory itself becomes the product, in addition to the specific good or service. In the experience economy, the customer builds an emotional tie with the organization. Like all of the other pillars in this book, the *welcome* pillar should guide *decisions* about the experiences people have with the school system.

While this may seem like just another business model forced onto schools, we do think that there is something to be said for our stakeholders' having an emotional tie with their learning environment. It is important to recognize that all members of the organization—not just students and their parents, but also teachers and administrators—are part of this emotional link and help create positive memorable experiences. In other words, the experience has a reciprocal relationship. Teachers cannot create an experience for students and not be touched by that experience themselves. Front office staff members cannot welcome guests without being transformed themselves. The experience economy is alive and well in schools where people feel welcome.

The Experience Economy Goes to School

A week after her interactions at the school and hotel, Nancy traveled to another school to observe a different student teacher. She walked into the front office where the school secretary and clerk were seated at a counter labeled "Concierge." Both immediately greeted her.

"How can I help you?" one woman offered. It was clear that their job at that moment was to make sure Nancy's needs and interests were attended to. When a student entered a few moments later, he turned to her and said, "Hi, I'm James. Welcome to our school." James was then greeted by the people at the front desk. Nancy couldn't help but notice that the boy received the same warm attention that Nancy had enjoyed. In reply, Nancy explained her task and offered her university identification, then asked where the classroom was located.

"Thank you, Dr. Frey. Could you please sign in to our guest book as well?" said the first woman as she handed her a pen. Nancy noticed that it was stuffed with pages of signatures and notes from other visitors that read like the ones she had seen in bed-and-breakfast establishments. "We'd love for you to write your comments in there before you leave this morning," the woman said.

"I'll take you to the classroom," offered the second woman at the desk. "It can get a little confusing."

As Nancy and the second woman crossed the campus, she witnessed many interactions between students and staff that seemed warm, casual, and genuine. Many staff members and students greeted her as James had, some introducing themselves and inquiring about her visit. Nancy entered her destination classroom with a bounce in her step. The positive memories of these experiences were converted into an equally positive and energetic observation and debriefing.

Later that day, Nancy told Ian about her amazing experience at the school and the regard she held for the people she had met. "It sounds like you were at the educational equivalent of a five-star resort," he observed. "It's not the opulence—it's the atmosphere."

"Teach a Man to Fish": The Role of Norms

Imagine if all staff members in your school considered it their job to make every student, parent, and visitor feel noticed, welcomed, and valued. We believe that school leaders must observe, model, coach, and expect this from each member of the school community. We believe systems can be designed and put in place to elicit these types of behaviors. The *welcome* pillar is the structure we use to organize the development of this cultural attribute in our schools. The effect on students is monumental. When students are immersed in a welcoming culture, they in turn sustain and extend that welcome to others.

It is worth repeating: Imagine if every staff member in your school considered it his or her job to make very student, parent, and visitor feel noticed, welcomed, and valued. How would that one single addition to each person's job description affect the culture of the school and the student achievement within it? Would more parents make choices to be our school partners? Would more visitors leave your site interested in creating that culture at their own schools? Would more students choose to come to school, choose to develop trusting relationships, and choose to actively engage in their education?

Experience Drives Choice

Have you ever asked yourself why people choose your school? It is a complex question that defies a simple answer. People buy houses in certain neighborhoods based on the school. Families of children who have struggled look for alternatives such as online academies, private schools, and homeschooling. Families are now being presented with more choices for determining where to send their children than ever before. Magnets, busing, inter- and intra-district enrollment policies, charters, vouchers, and homeschooling have increased the options that families can choose from when it comes to where their children will attend school.

And choice does not end there. How committed will the family be in their child's education? What efforts will families choose to make to help ensure their child's regular attendance, positive regard and success at school? Certainly these choices may be enhanced with family and school resources, and certainly choices will be constrained by an endless list of significant familial, financial, educational, and bureaucratic challenges. But in the end, and at any given point in time, families make choices about maximizing or minimizing their school involvement and support.

Ultimately, the choice of which school to attend comes down to the student. The choice for many students begins when it is time to get up each morning and whether they will go or not. It continues when they choose to leave home and stay on route to school instead of diverting toward the myriad of nonschool options presented by their interests, peers, or needs. Regardless of the procedures you have in place, students will also exercise some level of choice once they arrive at school. They will make choices to actually be where they are supposed to be and be there on time. Students will exercise this choice over and over again through the day, week, and year. Finally, and most importantly, students choose to engage or not, to tune in or not, to contribute or not, to value being in your school or not. We argue that school choice is really about the choices students make to attend your school physically, emotionally, and intellectually. The daily experiences that come from a welcoming environment and a commitment to consistency that builds the school community all influence the choices that students and their families make.

Attendance: Welcoming Those Who Aren't There

We've made a case that a welcoming environment is important, but the fact is that students with chronic attendance problems miss out on the culture we're all working so hard to achieve. To engage them in the learning environment, we have to find ways to get them to school and to intervene when they don't. To be sure, the root causes of chronic absenteeism are myriad and are influenced by health, child care, and family support systems. But schools committed to a welcoming culture are equally committed to finding ways to engage students and families in the importance of attendance. These efforts include

- Posting daily attendance percentages by grade level in a public and conspicuous place so that the entire school community knows if attendance goals are met.
- Sending "we missed you" cards in the mail, signed by teachers and administrators, each time a student is home sick.
- Hiring a paraprofessional or counselor to make home visits for each student who misses five days of school, not necessarily consecutively.
- Reporting to the police department or child protective services when students have excessive unexcused absences.
- Recognizing grade-level perfect attendance days with a variety of thank-you notes and awards.
- Meeting individually and weekly with 10 percent of students, those with the highest absence rates, to gain their commitment to attend school.
- Developing data-based goals for improving attendance, similar to those related to improving achievement.
- Sending recognition letters to students with exceptional attendance and to students who have made significant improvement in their attendance.

Consistency plays a vital part in these attendance interventions. Unless these efforts are applied each day, and with systems in place to trigger such responses, the job of getting students to the schoolhouse door crushes the few people who are made responsible for it. In a welcoming environment, each person in the organization plays a role in creating a positive culture.

Welcoming Some or All?

A number of years ago, Doug was working as a consultant to a district that had been mandated to increase the number of special education students in general education classrooms. He had been working with one high-achieving elementary school that was especially resistant to making any significant changes. The school often asked students to give visitors a tour, and on one of his visits a group of children met him in the front office. Doug asked them to show him the most important parts of their school. They took him first to the principal's office and then to the library. Both spaces were warm and inviting, with bright colors and lots of light. He then asked them "where the smart kids were," and they took him to the gifted classrooms on the campus. "I have a friend in there," one girl offered, pointing to the classroom door. The cultural capital of knowing someone in a gifted class was palatable. He then whispered, "Where are the stupid kids?" and they immediately led him to the self-contained special education wing of the school. "Are you friends with any of those kids?" he asked. "Not really," they replied. Not one of the caring adults at the school ever meant to teach children this lesson, and yet they had learned by observing the school's organizational structure that there was a fixed hierarchy of achievement in place, and that children should be sorted, even if it resulted in separation and isolation.

Doug's use of the word "stupid" was a pointed one, designed to determine whether this was indeed a part of the culture of the school. While shocking to adult ears, children use the word frequently to describe people, circumstances, and ideas. It is the language of children, and Doug posed the question as a way to enter their world. What was most telling was the children's lack of reaction to his question. Nothing would have thrilled Doug more if his guides had been confused or insulted.

Doug later shared this incident with the school's leadership team. The principal wept when she heard the story and made her own personal connection. Older members of her African American family had told her of their schooling experiences in the segregated South in the years before the Supreme Court's groundbreaking *Brown v. Board of Education* ruling put an end to this despicable practice in 1954. "It really isn't any different when you segregate out of a hatred or a misplaced sense of kindness," she said. "Separate is never equal, and it took our children to remind us of a lesson we should have learned decades ago." Within a year, every student with a disability at her school was enrolled in general education classrooms.

Upending Maslow's Hierarchy of Needs

In this chapter, we have applied several theories that emanate from the business world. But psychological and educational theories form the underpinnings of schooling. Abraham Maslow described motivation using a construct he called a hierarchy of needs (1943). He proposed that all humans have a series of needs, beginning with physiological ones such as food and water, safety needs such as health and security, and love and belonging needs that are met through friendship and family. Once met, higher levels of motivation such as esteem can be met through achievement and recognition. At the highest level is the self-actualization of a creative life.

School organizations are built to meet many of these needs, at least in theory. Breakfast programs, recess breaks, and safe and secure schools are all exemplars. But educational activist Norman Kunc challenges us to consider whether schools are really structured to meet *all* students' needs (2000). Kunc posits that in many schools the real structure is one that positions achievement as a condition of belonging. In other words, if you don't achieve, you are not able to reach membership and belonging. The result, however unintended, is a place where children point to where the "stupid" kids are. After all, they don't belong, and they aren't full members of the school community because they don't achieve in the same way.

A welcoming school community ensures that there is a place at the table for every member. This means that the school actively seeks opportunities to enact and extend inclusive practices. Students with and without disabilities participate as full members of classroom communities and learn alongside each other. Similarly, special and general educators work and learn with each other. The segregation of children often leads to a parallel segregation of faculty. In a welcoming environment, special educators don't opt out of mathematics professional development, and general educators don't refer to students with disabilities as "your kids."

Students with disabilities deserve the support that they need to achieve, and we in no way advocate for a "dump and hope" approach to inclusive practices. Like all other aspects of curriculum and instruction, inclusion needs to be purposeful and planned. This means making sure that general and special educators have opportunities to plan and work together, and that processes and procedures are developed to ensure that they have tools for communicating with one another beyond face-to-face interactions (Villa & Thousand, 2000). Additionally, this includes ensuring that the multifaceted supports that students with IEPs use are fully developed. We describe this as a triangle of supports: the personal, curricular, and technology systems that are uniquely combined to provide an education tailored to the needs of the student (Fisher, Sax, & Pumpian, 1999; Kennedy & Fisher, 2001).

Personal supports are those designed to provide students with the human resources that can make it possible for them to participate more fully in the learning and social life of the school. Depending on the needs of the student, these may range from the full-time support of a special education teacher or paraprofessional, to their part-time scheduled or intermittent support. These systems may also include formal peer supports or even the natural supports that occur within the classroom. In addition, related services personnel such as the speech/language pathologist may deliver services within the general education classroom.

Curricular supports are the accommodations or modifications needed for learning. Accommodations are often implemented and alter *how* a student receives information or demonstrates mastery of content. Examples of this include changing size of the assignment, changing the time allotted, or changing the form of a test from written to oral. Accommodations may also include changes to the input, such as listening to a recorded book. The Office of Special Education Programs makes more than 100,000 digital trade books available for free to students with disabilities. More information on this program can be found at www.bookshare.org. Modifications are generally reserved for students with intellectual disabilities and significantly change *what* the student is learning. Examples include narrowing the curriculum to focus on key points, or infusing functional IEP objectives into the school day, such as working on measuring skills for a student when the opportunity arises in chemistry.

Technology supports are those that increase communication and access through the use of specialized tools. These supports include assistive and augmentative communication devices, equipment that increases mobility, spelling checking and word prediction software, and even voice prompt recordings on a smartphone that provide verbal reminders to students to turn in homework or write down assignments in their agendas. Another example is a device called a smartpen, which allows a student to write notes on specially designed paper while recording the teacher's instruction. It can be played back at anytime whenever the pen touches the notes, providing the student with synchronized audio and visual information.

Taken together, a triangle of supports framework gives educators, students, and families a common vocabulary for articulating necessary supports to increase access and ensure membership in the community of learners. We have learned that this framework can be highly effective for students who are not yet performing at grade level, including students who are English-language learners. The framework complements effective instruction that continually allows us to remain open and willing to making the necessary changes that happen across the school year and not just during the annual IEP meeting. That willingness to take the time to be responsive is a foundational element of a welcoming culture.

"How Can I Help You? I Have the Time"

Sharp HealthCare, the largest public employer in San Diego, earned the coveted Baldrige award for performance excellence because they changed the healthcare *experience*. An organization does not receive a Baldrige award because of an incredible application, but because they demonstrate evidence that the system is consistently and progressively offering incredible experiences to the people served. Much of this work has directly influenced our thinking and practice. Who greets your visitors when they enter your campus? Will they feel special and welcomed? If not, it's time to consider some of the structures that should be in place to hardwire this pillar in the school.

Us and They

It should be clear from this pillar and our approach to building a student-centered culture that we believe the interactions and ensuing *relationships* that are typical in schools need to be rethought. We consciously attempt to redefine adult-to-adult, adult-to-student and student-to-student relationships. Administrators have different responsibilities than teachers and staff, yet all share a responsibility to operate a truly exceptional school. When teachers talk about administrators as "them" instead of as partners, boundaries prevent the transparent and collaborative flow of ideas, program development, and accountability. When we stand together every morning and revisit our mission by celebrating our success together, spotlighting students we will fortify resources around and events we all need to know about, we rekindle our mutual interdependence. We convey mutual respect and trust when any adult at any given moment volunteers to step up to support another. We spend more time on "us" as a team than on who is the boss and who is in the trenches.

Effective schools also try to blur the "us versus they" relationships between adult and student. Certainly, the professional responsibilities and ethics of each adult is a nonnegotiable, but the fact that we are all humans sharing a common interest in teaching, learning, and success creates a mutual accountability between adult and student. Our decisions to reduce and eliminate adult-only areas of the school, eating with students and making ourselves present and accessible for tutoring, mentoring, counseling, talking, and laughing with students, reduce the need to define relationships by power and authority alone.

Our attention to adult-to-adult and adult-to-student relationships based on common ground, respect, and mutual accountability also is intended to model how we expect students to treat each other. People feel *welcome* when "they" fades to "we" and everyone understands that there is a value in engaging in education together.

Fostering a Welcoming Culture with Service Cycles

John DiJulius (2008), an expert in what he calls world-class experiences, believes that service in America has never been worse, yet the experience economy suggests that service defines the competitive edge. We think DiJulius might come to similar conclusions about service in our schools, namely that it is not world-class and instead is putting us at competitive risk. His notion of creating "secret service behind-the-scenes systems" is the formula that the Ritz-Carlton relied on when employees greeted Nancy on her visit to the hotel. DiJulius defines secret service as "the implementation of hidden systems that enable our staff consistently to exceed clients' expectations and to make the client feel welcome, comfortable, important and understood" (2003, pp. 1–2). Imagine if our educational stakeholders had their expectations regularly exceeded and if they felt welcomed, comfortable, important, and understood each time they came to campus. Could a teacher want better conditions for learning and achievement than that?

The *welcome* pillar depends on leaders creating systems that facilitate organizational behavior and increase the likelihood that each staff member contributes to the authentic execution of that pillar. In promoting unforgettable experiences through secret service systems, DiJulius suggests that for every service we provide, there should be an agreed-upon customer service cycle. Each cycle requires an understanding and implementation of staff behaviors that range from general to detailed practice and from personal creativity to organizational principles. Using service cycles, DiJulius charts the customer's course from initial contact, to first visit, to repeat visit. He provides staff with activities and procedures for each step to increase the repeat visits. He emphasizes that these procedures will have similarities from service to service but will also have service-specific details that are responsive to the individual customer.

Analogous to DiJulius's customer service cycle, we believe that each educational stakeholder comes to the school with an agenda and our ability to welcome them and tailor our services to meet that agenda within the context of our mission requires the same agreed-upon service cycles of procedures, individual creativity, high touch, and organizational principles that make for successful organizations elsewhere. DiJulius measures the effectiveness of these systems in terms of repeat customers, where we would argue that educators should pursue these cycles with the intent of creating and sustaining student engagement. In other words, systems that increase the likelihood that students will enter school day after day expecting an amazing learning experience, and systems that let every visitor, parent, and vendor know that this school lives its mission and welcomes the productive dialogue and involvement of its stakeholders.

Organizational Principles

In creating a welcoming school culture, a number of organizational principles can be operationalized through service cycles. To start, we have provided principles we have found effective. Of course, each school will need to customize this list and develop principles that guide their work.

1. *Greet everyone with a smile and look at them.*
2. *Be present, and initiate and personalize conversations.*
3. *As you interact, ask the person what is going well and what he or she thinks needs to change.*
4. *Think about relationships that are based on respect and mutual accountability rather than on who is "us" and who is "them."*
5. *Provide an anticipatory mindset by understanding the person's agenda and giving an explanation when there is a delay.*
6. *Walk with people to their unfamiliar campus destinations (don't simply give directions).*
7. *Say thank you as often as you can.*
8. *Provide verbal and written communications to follow up as needed.*

9. *Have adults present in places frequented by students, not to supervise but to model how we greet and interact with others.*

10. *Teach and model understanding, respect, and tolerance.*

These 10 organizational principles guide the interactions we have with colleagues, visitors, and students. In addition, we see these as vital skills for students to learn so that they can communicate more effectively with each other and with adults on and off campus. In preparing students to be college- and career-ready, these principles of communication are intended to increase their skills at collaborating with a host of people to yield productive results.

Putting Principles into Action with Service Cycles

In our work with schools, we have often marveled at the truly innovative practices of individuals who raise the quality of experiences for students, teachers, and families on their campuses. We think, "That's a good idea!" but then forget about using the practice the next time the opportunity arises. Or we count on a procedure an individual uses year after year, one that really works, only to discover too late that when the person is no longer there, the procedure vanishes as well. Unfortunately, many school organizations rely on personality-driven innovations that disappear due to staff turnover or remain isolated because there is no mechanism for expanding their use. The purpose of service cycles in education is to codify institutional memory by cultivating innovative practices and developing these skills in others. In addition, it gives schools a mechanism for orienting new members of the school community to the culture of achievement developed over many years. These are service cycles that all schools can use in creating a welcoming culture and environment.

Welcoming routines for new students

Each year, schools welcome new students and their families into their schools. Some matriculate to a new campus from a feeder school, while others may be new arrivals to the community from another geographical location. By developing service cycles about how new students and families are welcomed into the school environment, you can create a positive first impression. These are especially important for students who enroll during the school year, as they are often left out of the important culture building that occurs during the first month. This is a sample outline for welcoming new students and families to your school:

• Outreach to future students and families
• Inquiries by the school are made by phone, email, or a visit
• Orientations and tours in advance of enrollment
• Application and enrollment procedures
• Follow-up contact with students who have enrolled

For instance, Harriet Tubman Middle School sends a welcome card to every new student enrolled in 6th grade, as well as those who will be joining the school for the first time as 7th and 8th graders. These cards are addressed to the student and welcome them to the school. In particular, the note inside expresses the excitement at the prospect of meeting the student and having them as a member of the community. Many schools already do this, but here's where Tubman staff have raised it to a new level. Principal Arlette Jackson explains that "every note is hand addressed and handwritten by a member of the staff. We have cards printed with the school's logo expressly for this purpose, and teachers and other staff add a short personal message and sign it. That way every new student receives a card from a specific person at the school.

She continued, "We mail these out about two weeks before school begins, when kids are starting to get nervous about attending a new school. We hear from students every year about how much they appreciated getting mail addressed to them, and not as a form letter with an address label stuck to it. You'd be surprised how seldom these children get personal mail," she chuckled. "But by doing this, we make sure students arrive here feeling like there is at least one person who's already made a personal connection with them." This is only one part of their service cycle for welcoming new students, and this middle school has found a way to make a lasting impression.

Welcoming routines for establishing a school culture

The work of a school culture is never achieved through a single assembly, field trip, or classroom activity. Rather, it is a living and breathing entity that must be actively tended to. After all, that's the premise of this book. However, it is essential that there are mechanisms in place to welcome students into the school's culture. The educators at Great Oaks Elementary School want all of their students to know that help is available for any variety of ordinary and extraordinary issues. From the first day of school, a team of 5th graders don red T-shirts emblazoned with SOS across the front, an acronym for "Students On Site." Their job is to be visible during the 30 minutes before school begins each day to direct students and families to locations in the school where assistance can be found, including the front desk, health clinic, and the guidance counselor's office. "They've been a great help," said assistant principal Roberto Ortiz. "I even see moms and dads go to the SOS children first because they have come to count on them as a way to direct them to resources." A service script establishing a welcoming culture includes the following:

- Public welcoming of students as they enter the school building
- Orientation to the building
- Learning about the staff and resources available
- Opportunities for students to learn about their classmates and teachers
- Opportunities for students to introduce themselves to classmates and teachers
- Cross-grade-level partnerships
- How to access assistance at school

At Health Sciences High and Middle College, we have invested lots of time and attention to the importance of this service cycle. Because our school year begins the Tuesday following Labor Day, our first week is just four days long. Unlike most schools, we devote this time to intensive culture building for all the students in the school. Throughout the first three days, students work in temporary grade-level groups to explore each of the pillars of the school's mission. They also meet in cross-grade-level groups for discussions about topics connected to the theme, called Paired Conversations. On the fourth day, the entire school participates in a field trip to a local park for a series of team-building activities with their Paired Conversation groups and then enjoys a barbeque. A number of other academic and procedural routines are also reserved for this time, which we call First Four Days (F4D).

Each year, a different pillar is spotlighted for further attention at F4D. For instance, a few years ago a cyberbullying incident occurred during the summer. Someone had established a "flame page" about a specific student on a social networking site and invited others to write anonymous mean-spirited comments about her. We knew nothing about this, but several students contacted Doug to alert him and ask what they could do to put a stop to it. (Fortunately, the targeted student knew nothing about the existence of the flame page about her.) He contacted the social networking site, and within 24 hours the flame page was deleted. However, the damage to our school's community had been done. When F4D occurred a few weeks later, the spotlighted pillar was Do No Harm (see more in chapter 3 about this pillar). Students learned about cyberbullying and the damage to an entire school community when any member is treated disrespectfully. Importantly, the themes and conversations established during this first week serve as a foundation for continued work throughout the year.

Welcoming routines for classrooms

A welcoming culture should permeate each day and should be just as obvious in mid-February as it was in early September. This means creating service cycles that exist within and around the academic routines of school. This can include teachers using "please" and "thank you" when giving directions, beginning each class with a warm greeting, and so on. A service cycle for classroom welcoming routines includes the following:

- Before class begins
- When class begins
- During instruction
- When class ends
- During transitions

Unfortunately, administrators and other nonclassroom personnel are overlooked in many schools when it comes to instructional involvement. This is especially true for those who are based in offices. At Madison High School, the entire staff has made a point of being present for students throughout the day. They have mutually committed to "be there" in the places where students gather. Therefore, before school, during passing periods, at lunch, and after school are dedicated times when people leave their offices and cubicles to be in the same places as students. "We call it 'prime time,'" joked technology coordinator Marlon Robinson. "Sometimes I'll lose track of time and someone will lean into my office door and say, 'Places, everyone'" While other pressing business may make it impractical for an individual to be present at a given time, the overarching practice is that adults are present. "It's not for supervision," said principal Arthur Ginsburg, "but it's surprising to see how often students will strike up conversations with adults in the school. Those small relationships can be a lifeline later for a student in crisis." By making sure that students feel welcome each and every day, schools like Madison are able to draw on a wider circle of support for all.

Welcoming routines for families

Throughout the school year, families meet with school personnel for a variety of reasons. In much the same way that we as consumers expect consistency in dealing with a large organization, families should expect the same treatment from us. While we often see school as grade levels and disciplines, families interact with a school across multiple years and view it as a single experience. After all, they may characterize an entire school through the lens of a single negative experience. "They never call you back at that school," they might say, even though the problem may have been with one teacher several years earlier. A service cycle of how we interact with families can help to bring consistency to this important process.

- Greeting
- Directing
- While waiting
- Beginning meetings
- Concluding meetings

- At time of departure
- Following up meetings through voice or written contact

The special education department at Tubman Middle School is a busy place. With nearly 150 students with disabilities enrolled in their large school, the number of IEP meetings with families is huge. But the special educators at Tubman are committed to making families feel welcome and valued at their school. Special education director Jessie Yee said, "After each meeting, the special educator writes a thank-you note to the family for attending. They usually say something about the value of their insights in helping us craft a good system of supports for their child. We got the idea from the welcome cards we send to new students each year," she remarked. "When we saw the positive reaction they sparked in students, we got together and figured we could do the same thing for families."

Welcoming routines for visitors

Throughout the day, visitors move through our buildings. Some are there to support teachers, as was Nancy as she conducted her university supervision of student teachers. Others are vendors, district maintenance personnel, and interested community members. Whether scheduled or unscheduled, anyone entering a place of business expects to be acknowledged and helped. Some are there for meetings and also have expectations about their interactions. Below is an example of a service cycle for visitors:
- Greeting
- Directing
- While waiting
- Beginning meetings
- Concluding meetings
- At time of departure
- Following up meetings through voice or written contact

Visitors often come to Great Lakes Elementary School to observe their educational practices. Several years ago, the school began displaying a welcome sign in a standing frame on the front counter of the main office that features the visitors' names and the date. "People are delighted when they come into the office and see their names on the welcome sign," said school secretary Alexandria Miller. "They feel like they were expected, and it just makes transitioning them to their destination that much easier. It also gives me a heads-up about whom to expect and where they will be heading." Visitors often remark that students will even know who they are. "I like to peek into the office every morning to see the names so I can say hi to them," said 4th grader Raymond Thomas. "They get so surprised when I say their name, and they want to know, 'How did you know that?' I tell 'em I'm psychic," he giggled.

Action Research Tools for Assessing a Welcoming Culture

Take a careful look around your school. Observe the interactions that are occurring. Determine who is really being *welcomed* and "primed" for a remarkable experience, and who is not. As you look around, do you feel the experience economy is in place and that it is engaging all of your stakeholders? As you reflect on what you see, think about ways this notion of *welcome*, service, and engagement could be enhanced by revisiting and reinvesting in the service cycles associated with the culture building of the *welcome* pillar. Each of the schools in this chapter uses action research as a way of calibrating its processes and refining its practices. These are necessary for ensuring that the welcoming experiences of the collective school community are maintained across the years. Here are some tools we recommend for beginning to look at how developed this aspect of your school culture is.

Secret shopper. This method of gauging customer services has been used for decades in retail environments and has been employed more recently as a means for examining the practices of nonprofit and service-oriented organizations such as places of worship, health care clinics, and social services agencies. Enlist a colleague who is not known at the school to approach the front desk as a visitor. Depending on the service cycle you would like to examine, this person can pose as a family member enrolling a new student, or perhaps a vendor. Using your service cycle as a checklist, the secret shopper can help you determine what processes are being implemented, as well as exposing any areas that might need improvement. Action research tool 4 is a sample secret shopper checklist for a person who is considering enrolling a new student.

Parent survey. Action research tool 5 is a sample survey that can be used to collect data from family members about their experience with the school. We are particularly interested in the perspective that family members have about how they are treated when they visit the school and how the school communicates with them, and in what formats. As with the other action research tools in this book, using the action research cycle means that you will synthesize the data from this survey and identify strengths and weaknesses. These can be added to your SWOT analysis (action research tool 3) and be used to determine professional development needs and interventions. For example, if the data from this survey suggest that administrators are not easy to talk to, then you'll have to think about what that means, and then take action to change that aspect of the school's welcoming culture. Of course, the actions should be followed with another round of data collection to determine if the actions had an effect or not. The second round of data collection and analysis will likely suggest additional areas to think about and act upon.

Student focus groups. Action research tool 6 is the student focus group, an important tool for gathering the opinions and impressions of a group of people regarding the qualitative aspects of a service. In marketing, this tool is often used to gather impressions of a product. You may have been approached at a shopping mall to participate in a focus group. It is essential to note that focus groups are carefully constructed to capture a broad range of consumers. Therefore, student focus groups should also be selected to include students who are likely to have different experiences. To gauge the quality of the welcoming culture at your school, include students who have attended for several years, as well as those who are newer. In addition, be sure that the groups are not skewed so that the only voices that are heard belong to high-achieving students who have never had any conflict with the school. Because participants are likely to slant their reported opinions based on what they believe the interviewer wants to hear, an objective third-party interviewer should be enlisted for this task. In addition, be sure to design the questions you use so that they are not leading. Action research tool 7 is an interview form for students about a welcoming culture and environment.

Conclusion

We believe these welcoming experiences are part and parcel to creating a culture for learning because it is a culture that promotes positive choices. Simply stated, people will choose to be engaged in and with your school. We are convinced that the same experience-oriented cultures that drive success in business can lead to student achievement and success in school.

How far into a school or classroom can a student or parent get before they are greeted and welcomed by anyone? How many adults can a student walk by before the student is recognized? Does the level of frustration of an angry parent or scared student increase or dissipate with each step they take in your school?

The experience we try to create every day is one that is the educational equivalent of a five-star resort. And it's not the opulent furnishings that make a difference, but rather the sense of belonging and membership that is extended to everyone. Effective schools, like effective organizations, do not leave these dreams to chance. Leadership is needed, and systems need to be designed and put into place and managed. The emotional intelligence of the organization needs to be fine-tuned so all stakeholders feel welcomed and, in turn, commit to teaching, learning, developing, and achieving.

CHAPTER 3

Do No Harm

There may be no better way of examining the culture of a school than to hold informal conversations with students. If you take the time, students will offer you honest and often raw insights into their school's culture. While serving as an interim middle school principal, Ian invited a group of 8th graders for a chat. "I'm curious," he started, "if any of you have ever been sent to the principal's office because you got in trouble for what you thought was a dumb reason?" One quickly responded, "Chewing gum dumb enough for you? I mean, really, are you kidding me?"

"Who was it?" asked another.

"Berkowitz."

"There you go!" said the second student. "You can't chew gum in her class."

Ian asked, "Isn't it a school rule that you can't chew gum?"

"Well, you can and you can't. It depends whose class you're in."

Ian said, "You mean you could give me a list, class by class, where you can and cannot chew gum?"

"Sure, I mean, we can even tell you which teachers chew it themselves," another said.

"And *I* get sent to the principal's office!" said the first student.

Ian responded, "What did the principal tell you?"

"If I get sent out of class again, I'll get in-school suspension!"

The students went on to list a host of other "dumb reasons" they had been sent to the office: uniform violations, being late for class, failure to have a pencil and paper, having a cell phone. Finally, Ian asked them what was the most important thing they had learned about the school's rules.

"You need to know when and where you can't do stuff, because some teachers pay more attention to the rules than other ones do," one said. Out of the mouths of babes.

Your processes and procedures should be tools for teaching students to become the moral and ethical citizens you expect them to be. Furthermore, rules should be viewed as a single tool, but not the only one, for doing so. Reread your student handbook. Look at what you are expecting, and think about whether it conveys your mission in the preparation of a responsible citizenry. Is it a catalog of rules, or does it represent your school's mission of a commitment to learning?

It is interesting to examine the relationship between safe schools and achievement. Steinberg, Allensworth, and Johnson (2011) analyzed survey data from more than 130,000 students and teachers in Chicago Public Schools and found that the perception of a safe and orderly environment was more strongly influenced by what occurred within the school than in the immediate neighborhood around it, and that the best predictor of the school's safety was the achievement of the students within it. They also reported that as a school's suspension rate rose, students felt *less* safe, and further noted that "disadvantaged schools with high-quality relationships feel as safe as advantaged schools with weak relationships" (p. 43). The authors went on to say,

> The nature and quality of the interactions between adults and students matter greatly. But positive interactions do not just happen organically. Promoting positive interactions between students and adults requires concerted attention to the ways in which the school environment is structured. For example, training teachers and staff on how to deal with conflict in constructive ways could help prevent conflicts from escalating. (p. 3)

Learning can't happen at a significant level in a school that is out of control. And the intent of the *do no harm* pillar is to increase the positive behavioral profile of the school in order for teachers and students to do what they do best: learn together.

The *Do No Harm* Pillar

No single topic, save grading, divides a staff and defines a school more than how it approaches rules and discipline. But the fact is that rules don't teach students to behave—people do. So you might be tempted to ask, "What are the purposes of our school's rules?" It's really the wrong question to start with, because it will quickly lead to discussions about details like gum chewing and whether we will allow it and whether we can enforce it. But what if you began your discussion by asking about the purposes of education? What is your mission, and what sort of behaviors would be exemplars of that mission among your graduates? Does creating a list of rules that will be inconsistently and sporadically enforced help teach students about making responsible choices and doing the right thing? These are the essential questions regarding the *do no harm* pillar. This pillar puts adults in the position of teaching students to assess their actions as appropriate or not based on an ethical standard and not simply adherence to a set of rules that are subjectively judgmental and too often inconsistently enforced.

Free at Last, but to Do What?

Ian took his son Eli and his friends out for dinner when he picked Eli up at the end of his freshman year at the University of Oregon. The friends were sharing stories about surviving the dorms and their coursework. They also talked about their peers who didn't make it through the year. Ian asked, "What was different about you guys? Why did you make it, but they didn't?"

The conversation was fascinating. They said most of the guys who didn't make it came from schools and homes where rules were used to control behavior. When those students arrived at the university, they had little experience at setting their own limits on new freedoms, and they couldn't handle it. Their irresponsibility caught up with them in the form of missed classes, failing grades, and disciplinary committee actions. In comparison, Eli and his friends spoke of coming from schools and homes where they were given reasonable levels of freedom and taught to behave responsibly, rather than being denied privileges for every infraction. No doubt, the parents and high school teachers of the guys who were no longer at the university had presumed that compliance demonstrated responsibility and self-control. Although compliance represents respect for an external locus of control, it may not result in learning to develop one's internal locus of control.

Do as I Say, Not as I Do?

On the first day of a graduate class that Ian was teaching, the teachers were asked to share what they believed were their most important classroom rules. Little did they know their college professor was going to use this informed list to propose the class's operational norms. The first teacher chimed in that she felt being on time was a fundamental class rule, no excuses. The next teacher shared his insistence that his students come prepared for class.

"What about PDAs?" asked Ian, to which he quickly got consensus from the group that cell phones and PDAs were confiscated if used in class. In fact, in most classrooms and schools, electronics were not allowed to be out or used during school hours. One of the teachers said she marked off a full letter grade for all homework turned in late. Two middle school teachers proclaimed that adherence to a school uniform policy was a fundamental means of promoting school achievement.

Ian recorded the list of these rules passed down by experienced professional educators and suggested that the class should review the list, because they would now be the norms for this graduate class experience. Over the course of the semester, they challenged this set of rules and began to discuss alternatives. A few examples of the rules, and discussions about them, follow.

Better late than never... but better never late. What is the harm in being late? It depends. If you are late for a plane, it can cost you a great deal. If you are chronically late for a job, you will likely get bad reviews and eventually it might cost you a job. Late for a movie or play, and you might be lost the rest of the evening. Late for class or a meeting, your participation will be limited, and you might miss essential information or a critical decision. A pattern of unexplained tardiness can be considered rude or disrespectful. Punctuality is a desired virtue and demonstrates a level of organizational competence and public respect.

The teachers in the graduate seminar agreed that being on time, no exceptions, was a class rule that should be followed with consequences. "So," Ian asked, "is being on time to our class a reasonable class rule?" Yes, they responded, but you need to realize we have busy lives, we are coming here after a day of teaching, we often have meetings at school, or my kid has a Wednesday Little League game that will make me late. And what if parking is a problem?

Kerry was the teacher who first proposed that being to class on time was a fundamental class rule. While she was explaining her rationale, three teachers entered the classroom and sat down. Although no one in the class found their 20-minute late arrival to be unusual or disrespectful, Margo did comment on this. She said, "Being on time is a standard we should teach, support, encourage, and respect." But what standard should we use for that expectation? What excuses, if any, might we care to hear, and what should be the response or consequences for a student's being tardy?

Taylor relayed a story about a student named Wendy who arrived late to school every single day. First period started at 8:00 a.m. and she would arrive somewhere between 8:45 and 9:10. Her teachers talked about the material she was missing and the lack of concern and respect she was demonstrating. She seemed unaffected by the talks that several teachers and administrators had had with her. Finally, someone sat down and really got a sense of Wendy's morning. She got up every day at 6:00 a.m. and helped get her two younger siblings dressed, fed, and off to school. She boarded a bus that took her downtown where she transferred to another bus that got her to school. She had chosen the school to escape the pressure of drugs and gangs her friends were involved with in her neighborhood. While everyone had presumed her tardiness was a sign of disrespect and apathy, the fact that she went through a three-hour routine every morning to get to school made her among the school's most committed students. Instead of punishing and threatening her, Taylor reported that the school refocused efforts to create some acknowledgment, flexibility, and accommodation.

Come prepared. When Juan shared his expectation that students had to be ready when class started with pencil or pen in hand, Ian could not help thinking that he had borrowed a pen and paper from one of the teachers 10 minutes earlier to take attendance and no one thought to berate him or ask him to leave. In fact, Ian is not proud of the fact that somewhere between his car and every meeting he seems to misplace his pen, paper, or reading glasses. And everywhere he goes, his colleagues, students, and even strangers are willing to lend him a pen, give him paper, share an agenda, and even locate an extra pair of reading glasses.

Coming prepared to class, a meeting, or any of a wide range of social and professional activities is a desirable virtue. By all accounts, however, if coming prepared with paper and pen to class or meetings was an absolute determinant of success, Ian should be a complete failure. But to the contrary, most would consider Ian's professional achievements and contributions admirable despite his lack of pen-and-paper behaviors. Yes, we want to teach, encourage, and expect students to come prepared to class, but again what standard should be absolutely applied and at what consequence? Principal Sheri North decided that she never wanted a student sent to the office again because he or she did not have a pencil. So Doug came up with a simple solution for Sheri. Every couple of months, she buys a few thousand golf pencils and encourages each teacher to keep a box in their classrooms. This solution does not substitute the need to teach students to come to school prepared, but it does reframe the agenda and keeps students from missing class for lack of a pencil.

No multitasking here. Have you ever watched a great bartender work? There is no wasted movement. Drinks are poured, glasses are cleaned, stock is reshelved, credit cards are processed, and multiple conversations are simultaneously held up and down the counter with grace. It is so impressive. We see the same fluidity when we walk into the classrooms of master teachers. Undoubtedly we expect airplane control engineers to monitor multiple planes in the air at the same time, nurses to keep track of the orders for of multiple patients, and a broker to manage several customer portfolios simultaneously. Multitasking in the real world is not punished; it's rewarded and revered. Only when work is sloppy or attention is disrespectful do we question whether someone is managing too many things at once. In those situations, we provide comment, advice, or intervention.

"No cell phones or PDAs in my class—that is a nonnegotiable for me," stated Michael, a 7th grade English teacher in the graduate class. Upon hearing Michael's contribution, another student looked up from his smartphone. He had been texting confirmation of his flight times, and delaying that text would have been problematic for the colleagues who needed to make arrangements to pick him up the next day. Similarly, several other teachers had checked their messages before, during, and soon after Michael's comments but generally supported the no electronics class rule. Others were on their personal laptops, managing to concurrently take class notes and answer email. Can you remember one staff meeting in the last year when you have not witnessed a similar scene? Of course not, because we are capable of multitasking, or continuous partial attention, and our crazy lives require that we do it often.

We do feel that students need to learn how to manage the use of their electronic devices in a way that supports, or at least does not interfere with, their classroom performance and participation. That is clearly possible for most of us. We also have learned when multitasking will be counterproductive to the task at hand, and hopefully we learn when to put it aside. Most of all, students need to learn to use these devices in a manner that is respectful. At some schools, a courtesy policy that is designed to support the polite use of technology takes the place of a prohibition policy (see figure 3.1).

If teachers believe PDAs or MP3 players are being used in a manner that is disruptive and disrespectful, students are confronted with the school's courtesy policy. If it is to prepare students for life, then we have to teach, reinforce, and tolerate responsible use of technology. Of course it would be easier to exercise your ultimate authority and control by just preventing cell phones and music in school, but you will be creating a culture far removed from the one that students value and far away from the world they will need to thrive in as adults.

These examples from the graduate class experience suggest that hard and fast rules, applied to all situations, are difficult to enforce. They are also of questionable utility because these rules require that adults assume the position of power and apply rewards and consequences based on student behavior. How different could schools be if students regulated their own behavior? How would the roles of teachers, students, parents, and administrators change as a result? And how can a culture be created that supports student self-regulation? The key idea that we have come to understand is this: *Rules don't teach responsible and ethical behavior. People do.*

FIGURE 3.1
Sample Courtesy Policy

Courtesy is a code that governs the expectations of social behavior. Each community or culture defines courtesy and the expectations for members of that community or culture. As a learning community, it is our responsibility to define courtesy and to live up to that definition. As a school community, we must hold ourselves and one another accountable for interactions that foster respect and trust. Discourteous behaviors destroy the community and can result in hurt feelings, anger, and additional poor choices.

In general, courtesy means that we interact with one another in positive, respectful ways. Consider the following examples of courteous and discourteous behavior.

Courteous	Discourteous
• Saying please and thank you • Paying attention in class • Socializing with friends during passing periods and lunch • Asking questions and interacting with peers and teachers • Asking for, accepting, offering, or declining help graciously • Allowing teachers and peers to complete statements without interruptions • Throwing away trash after lunch • Cleaning your own workspace • Reporting safety concerns or other issues that require attention to a staff member	• Using vulgar, foul, abusive, or offensive language • Listening to an iPod during a formal learning situation such as during a lecture or while completing group work • Text messaging or talking on a cell phone during class time when the teacher is talking or you are working in a group • Bullying, teasing, or harassing others • Not showing up for your scheduled appointments or completing tasks • Failing to communicate when you're not coming to school

Self-Regulation: Fostering a Culture of *Do No Harm*

Most school systems operate on a behaviorist system of rewards and pun-ishments. But do behaviorist systems result in long-term change, especially in the absence of the person providing the rewards and consequences? As Costello, Wachtel, and Wachtel (2009) note, "punishment only works when the authority is watching" (p. 77). This places school staff in an awkward position of having to continually police the environment. Albert Bandura (1986) was not satisfied with what he saw as a simplistic view of learning, based totally on the environment and that which was observable. He did not believe that the behaviorist theory was making use of two of the things that make humans unique: observational learning (modeling) and self-regulation.

It is now widely accepted that humans learn through observation or modeling. This includes several components, including:

- **Attention**: If humans are to learn something, they have to pay atten-tion. If something restricts attention—fatigue, stress, drugs—learning is reduced.
- **Retention**: If humans are to remember something, they have to retain what they paid attention to. These memories are stored as visual and linguistic representations. These mental images and verbal descriptions can later be retrieved so that the person can reproduce them with their own behavior.
- **Reproduction**: When the mental images and verbal descriptions are implemented, they become behavior. Prior to this, they're ideas. Impor-tantly, the behavior is also based on skill. Watching a professional dancer does not mean that you can dance the same way. But if you have the skills as a dancer, you will be able to perfect your craft when you observe others.
- **Motivation**: Even if you can engage in the behavior, you may or may not choose to do so based on your motivation. Motivation comes in many forms, including past reinforcements, promised reinforcements, and vicarious reinforcements. According to Bandura, these are not the causes of behavior, as behaviorism would suggest, but rather demon-strations of our learning. In addition, there are negative motivations

which include past punishment, promised punishments, and vicarious punishments. All of these factors are operating as students acquire new behaviors.

The second part of Bandura's theory focuses on self-regulation, another uniquely human trait and one that could not be observed in studies by Pavlov on dogs or Skinner on pigeons. Self-regulation, controlling our own behavior, has three components, according to Bandura:

- **Self-observation**: We observe ourselves, and we keep track of our behavior.
- **Judgment**: We compare what we see in our own behavior with a standard for behavior. This standard is one that we have accepted for our comparison, such as the culture of a school or rules in the family or expectations for etiquette.
- **Self-response**: The comparison of our behavior with the standard results in self-rewards or self-punishing. It is the automatic response we have when we compare our behavior with the standard we set for ourselves. These can be obvious, as in treating yourself to a movie, or covert, as in feeling pride or shame.

In terms of personality, self-regulation is related to self-concept, which is better known today as self-esteem. If, over time, you find your behavior meeting the standard you set, you will have a positive self-concept and good self-esteem. If, on the other hand, you find your behavior lacking, below standards, you will develop a poor self-concept and have low self-esteem. One caution that Bandura offers relates to the standard itself. Setting the standard too high will result in failure and poor self-concept.

This has significant implications for schools. What it says to us is that one arbitrary rule will not apply for all students. As with instruction, we have to scaffold our behavioral expectations. Although the goal can be the same, the standard we set and teach might differ from one student to another. We are reminded of a student who was very difficult behaviorally. When Nancy met with her privately, the girl stated that she did not really see any problem with her behavior. In Bandura's words, her self-observation and judgment, based on the standard she had set for herself, were in concert and her self-concept was strong. She did not see that using foul language, arguing publicly with teachers, arriving late to all of her classes, or leaving class when she needed to were problematic at all. In her words, "Why you gotta be in my business? I hadta go and take care of things." When asked about her interaction with a teacher, she said, "Yeah, I don't like it when they talk back to me, so I tell them what is."

The standard this student set for herself, one that was observed at home, was not acceptable at school. But telling her the rules and then punishing her for breaking them had not worked in her previous years of schooling. Instead, Nancy recognized that this would be a slow process and one that would require a redefinition of the standard of behavior. Critically, Nancy recognized that the student had to own these new standards and that starting with standards that were too high would result in immediate failure. If you're wondering, this student has radically changed her behavior and is on track to graduate. She still has bad days, especially related to her home life, but as her English teacher said, "She's so interesting, filled with good ideas waiting to get out. She just needs a little space now and then." Who would have guessed that the student who was suspended 19 times in 8th grade would have a teacher say that about her?

Bandura's recommendations for addressing behavioral challenges can be clustered into three main areas. As you will see later in this chapter, these are also part of the work being done under the label *restorative practices*. In general, the goal is to invite students to reconsider their standards of behavior, monitor their behavior, and make changes along the way. In doing so, we have to be sure that we do not ostracize, shame, or exclude students based on their behavior. In fact, the goal of our self-regulation efforts should be to integrate the student as soon as possible after the situation has been addressed because we understand that the environment causes behavior *and* that behavior causes environment. Bandura labeled this concept reciprocal determinism, noting that both of these factors, behavior and environment, play a role in the learning that occurs. The specific actions Bandura recommended include:

- **Behavioral charts**: These are visual displays of behavior, albeit personal and not public. This can include an occurrence list, journal, or checklist. The idea is to keep track of the details, including when, where, and why, the behavior occurred. A sample behavioral chart for a 3rd grader working to manage his outbursts in class can be found in figure 3.2. This tool is used for each occurrence of an outburst, and the student has been taught to select at least one response from each column.

- **Environmental planning**: After analyzing the behavioral chart, the student is assisted in analyzing the chart, as needed. Although some students do not need help analyzing their behavioral charts, the conversation that a caring adult can have about the behavioral patterns is often useful. The analysis should provide the student with an idea of the actions he or she can take to avoid the behavior, including the removal of triggers or antecedents or the development of coping mechanisms following a specific stimulus. The 3rd grader met briefly with a counselor each day to talk about his observations of his own behavior, and she worked with him to process both positive and negative incidents to help him gain insight.

- **Self-contracts**: These are written and signed agreements with yourself to change your behavior and include the consequences and rewards for breaking or meeting the terms of the contract. These are often witnessed by school staff, but they are developed by the student, with assistance from a trusting adult, based on the analysis of behavioral charts and environmental planning. For example, a behavioral contract developed by a middle school student, with the assistance of a teacher he trusted, included the following:

  - Put forth effort in every class and engage in lessons and activities designed by the teacher. I have demonstrated my ability to complete my work and earn passing grades and will make sure that this continues to happen.
  - Show respect to my teachers by promptly and politely responding to their class directions and rules—this includes using choice words in class. I know there are a number of adults who I can go to outside of

class time who will help me when I have an issue I want to discuss. I know that this includes a restorative practice conversation to let me tell other people how their actions affected me.

♦ Attend lunchtime tutoring EVERY DAY for 30 minutes until all of my grades are C or better. My attendance in tutoring will be logged by a weekly attendance log that is signed off by a tutor.

♦ Failure to meet the terms of this contract will result in my not being allowed to have electronic devices in any classroom or in the hallways at school.

FIGURE 3.2
Sample Behavioral Chart

This chart is for you to keep track of when you are calling out answers or arguing with someone. When that happens, ask yourself what your reason was. You can circle more than one answer. You can talk about these reasons with Ms. DeLeong next time you meet with her.

What happened?	How did others react?	What was your reason?	What else could you have done?
Called out an answer	They ignored me.	I knew something and I wanted to share it.	Wait
Called someone a name	They looked angry.	I wanted someone to stop doing something.	Ignore
Argued with someone	They laughed.	I wanted someone to start doing something.	Ask for help
Kept talking after I was asked to stop	They did what I wanted them to do.	I wanted someone to pay attention to me.	Move to a different part of the room
What else do you want to say about this? Would you do the same thing again?			

The place we want to get to is one in which the culture of the school becomes the standard by which an individual judges his or her behavior. A school culture should be a living example of a place where people, both adults and children, take responsibility for their interactions and make amends when they interfere with the well-being of others. We want to move away from reprimands and toward self-regulation. In other words, we want to put more energy into being proactive and preventative, rather than having to spend our days reacting to each infraction that occurs.

A *Do No Harm* Culture Is Preventative

A responsive school culture should first seek to prevent harm to others through measured words and behaviors. The *do no harm* pillar was designed to reframe the whole discussion about the ways in which policies, procedures, and rules about behavior affect students. Like all of the other pillars, it is also intended as a way of framing what students learn. For students to develop their capacity to self-regulate, they need a standard that is conducive to the school. We define this standard across three dimensions:

- Take care of yourself.
- Take care of each other.
- Take care of this place.

Collectively, these describe the positive behaviors that are needed in learning and, we would argue, in life. These also afford a way to have conversations with students about examples and nonexamples of each.

- In her 10th grade health classroom, Annaleah Enriquez uses her lesson on the destructive skin-cutting practices of troubled adolescents as an example of self-harm, and she provides resources for ways that a student can seek help at school and in the community.
- In his kindergarten classroom, Paco Flores teaches a lesson using a paper doll, crushing it as he recites some of the verbal taunts used by 5-year-olds. He discusses the harm inflicted on others when they hear, "Go away—you can't play with us." He then asks students about ways to fix this and smoothes the paper doll while they say things like, "We're

sorry." After praising them for making amends, he points out that the "scars" (wrinkles) remain even after the apologies (Katz, Sax, & Fisher, 2003).

- In her 7th grade physical science classroom, Meghan Greb praises her students as they clean up and put away the materials they used for their recently completed lab experiment, reminding them, "This is a great way to take care of this place—thank you!"

We are not sure how many of the rules each student can recite in the signed copies of the student handbook, but this proactive culture begins the first day with a declaration of our commitment and expectation to *do no harm*. We introduce these as standards during our First Four Days activities (see chapter 2 for more details) so that they are equipped to compare their behavior against something. At the end of the first week of school, students can tell you that the purpose of every school rule is to *do no harm* to yourself, to others, and to the environment so that learning can take place. In keeping with both a welcoming culture and one that attempts to prevent harm from occurring, we also use a practice that places caring adults in the places where support is likely to be needed.

Hallway TLC

Observe the traffic in your school's hallways during class and note who is out and why. Some students are traveling purposefully from one place to another, perhaps the library or computer lab. But there are others who are the frequent fliers of the halls. They always seem to be going to or coming from the bathroom, or they're headed to the nurse's office with a vague complaint. Perhaps they've got that listless gait that telegraphs the dread they feel about returning to class. Some of these students are likely to be in quiet crisis. The girl with the seemingly small bladder is really headed there so she can answer the text her mom sent about a family member's troubles. The boy with the stomachache is worried about the argument his parents had that morning. The child shuffling his feet is trying to time his arrival so that he misses his turn to read aloud in front of the class.

Students who demonstrate their unhappiness in obvious ways gain our immediate attention. In the meantime, the quietly despairing are overlooked, at least until they explode later. And in too many cases, students who have sought the temporary refuge of a quieter place are greeted by a security guard who is pointing with his walkie-talkie while growling, "Where's your pass?" Unfortunately, this can be the trigger for a downward spiral of problematic behavior—all without the underlying issue ever being addressed.

Several years ago we began a practice we call Hallway TLC (tender loving care). (We have to thank Sharp HealthCare for inspiring this.) We place a table and two chairs in a busy area of the school under a sign that says, "Hallway TLC: How can I help you? I have the time." Any adult can sit there for any length of time. Sometimes we'll find a teacher using 10 minutes of his prep period to staff the table, or an administrator who has relocated her computer there to finish a report. Sometimes no one is there, because we don't adhere to a strict staffing schedule. The important thing is understanding what it is and is not. Adults are not there to supervise, but rather to be watchful and available. The key is to have a second empty chair for anyone who needs to use it. It can be an invitation: "Come sit here with me. You look like something's troubling you." At other times, students will see a trusting adult at the table and sit right down voluntarily. The boy whose parents fought this morning might just need to have an ordinary conversation with a friendly adult. We don't treat Hallway TLC as a confessional, but rather as a release valve. The student who's delaying his return to the reading table would benefit from a follow-up conversation with his teacher. The girl with the family troubles might need the skills of a counselor. The intent of Hallway TLC is to be proactive—to get ahead of a looming crisis by providing support and encouragement. Sometimes it's even another adult who will take advantage of the chance to share a personal issue with a caring colleague. While this practice doesn't prevent all crises, it has been fruitful in finding ways to locate supports in the places that students frequent.

Spending time at the Hallway TLC table also gives you a glimpse of who might need more intensive support. A student who is a frequently in the chair may need a counseling or health referral. This process shouldn't supplant the other good supports and services offered by a school, but it can help students with mild and transient problems while steering students in crisis to more lasting supports.

One of the most profound experiences we had with Hallway TLC involved a young man who habitually spent quite a bit of time in the hallways. He wasn't the type who caused trouble, but he did always seem to have one reason or another for not being in class. On one of his many self-initiated breaks, he spied Doug sitting at the table. After looking both ways to see if anyone was within earshot, he said quietly, "Can I sit in the talking chair?" He chose that time and place to confess that he had been using illegal drugs to self-medicate and needed help. This student's journey to recovery would be a long one and certainly couldn't be resolved with a bit of small talk. But the first step to getting him the assistance he would need from his family and from trained professionals began in Hallway TLC. "Thanks for trusting me enough to tell me that," Doug told him. "I promise we'll always have the time."

When Harm Is Done

Think about a time when a student caused harm. It doesn't have to be physical harm; it could be harm to the learning community or something like that. The instinct we all have is to punish offenders. We want to know that there are consequences for transgressions against accepted rules. We want assurances that the student will pay the price for the offense. Typically, we think about the consequences for students along a continuum between punitive and permissive, something that looks like this:

<--->

Punitive   Neutral   Permissive

This continuum suggests that there is a range of consequences for each problem behavior. Corporal punishment, detention, suspension, and expulsion are at the punitive end of the scale. In the middle might be loss of privileges, and further to the right, a scolding—or even ignoring the issue altogether.

But then ask yourself, are the consequences we have available to us actually working? Is another suspension going to change the fact that Brandon does not see the effect of his behavior on others? Will locking out students who are late to school teach them to be on time? Is expelling Marla providing her with a learning opportunity or shifting the responsibility to teach her respect to someone else? That's not to say that suspensions and expulsions are never appropriate. There are some conditions that must be dealt with swiftly and decisively. But the majority of situations that occur daily in schools do not fall under this category. And most of the major events that happen in school can be traced to ineffective practices from previous years.

We also don't believe that ignoring a problematic behavior will work any better than punishment and consequences. We do think that action should be taken when students do harm, whether that be to themselves, others, or the environment. But that action has to hold students accountable in a way that helps them understand the effect their behavior has on others. We are particularly taken with the idea of restorative practices, which has its roots in the New Zealand's restorative justice movement (Maxwell & Liu, 2007). The goals of restorative practices include the following:

- Trying to foster understanding of the impact of the behavior
- Seeking to repair the harm that was done to people and relationships
- Attending to the needs of victims and others in the school
- Avoiding imposing on students intentional pain, embarrassment, and discomfort
- Actively involving others as much as possible (Costello et al., 2009, p. 52)

Engaging in restorative practices changes the situation from a linear continuum between punitive and permissive actions to one focused on support and control. As demonstrated in the social discipline window (figure 3.3), high control and low support is punitive whereas low control and high support is permissive. In other words, the continuum only provides two options, to do things *to* students or *for* them. There are other options. With low control and low support, students are *not* accountable, and the adults have abdicated their responsibility to guide learning. The fourth quadrant is where we'd like to be. We can engage *with* students and create restorative opportunities, which allow them to meet the goals identified on page 55.

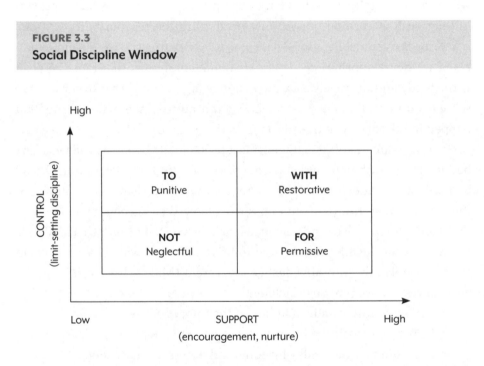

FIGURE 3.3
Social Discipline Window

Source: Costello, B., Wachtel, J., & Wachtel, T. (2009). *Restorative practices handbook for teachers, disciplinarians and administrators.* Bethlehem, PA: International Institute for Restorative Practices. P. 50, used with permission.

To implement restorative practices requires that the adults in a school believe that "decisions are best made and conflicts are best resolved by those most directly involved in them" (Costello et al., 2009, p. 7). Anyone who has spent time in school knows that this is not routinely done. When a student misbehaves, he or she is sent to an administrator. Most likely, the student sits in a chair in the front office waiting to be seen. When the time finally comes for the offender to see the administrator, the student has likely calmed down and has a reasonable conversation. The administrator applies a punishment and asks for a commitment from the student not to do that again. Then the student returns to the classroom, unlikely to change his or her behavior next time. It amounted to little more than the teacher and student taking a break from each other's company.

Of course, there are even less effective courses of action. One of the mistakes often made is to ask the student, "WHY did you do that?" Chances are, he or she really doesn't know. The conversation won't get anywhere in terms of learning, but it might result in a rationalization or justification of the behavior, which could result in the behavior being seen as acceptable. Bandura would call this setting a new standard. Another ineffective approach is to force an apology, which simply builds resentment in the person required to apologize as a condition of earning membership back into the group. Remember, the student is aware of the standard and is evaluating that standard all of the time. When students believe that they have met their standard yet are forced to apologize, it's not going to be sincere and the receiver of the apology will know that. The only person likely to feel any satisfaction is the adult who was forcing the apology out of the guilty party.

That's not to say that apologizing is wrong; indeed, it is a significant part of restorative practices. But it can only occur when the offender is ready to apologize based on an understanding that harm has been done and that the goal is to repair the relationships. In fact, it might be better to ask the student, "What can you do to make things right?" rather than force an apology. This will allow you to assess the student's thinking about his or her behavioral standard and to determine if the standard has been met. If the student does not think that anything needs to be done to make things right, there is more work to be done relative to expectations and standards.

To build the culture of *do no harm*, adults and peers must respond when harm is done. As we have noted previously, it is important that the culture be built such that the majority of students, most of the time, choose the culture of the school as their standard. In doing so, they monitor their own behavior and make choices about how they want to act. This requires that the adults and students in a building have a strong relationship. The tone must be positive, and the adults must learn to "separate the deed from the doer" (Costello et al., 2009, p. 63) making it clear that the behavior is unacceptable but the person is valued. There are a number of implementation components for restorative practices, which we will discuss next. Restorative practices require the development of relationships—trust—and will not work if students only ever have these types of conversations when they have caused harm. The basis of this model is in the affective statements all of the adults in the school use. This aspect will be addressed further in the chapter focus on the pillar *choice words*, but it is also critical to the implementation of restorative practices. In addition, when harm has been done, whether that be to others, self, or the environment, we start with affective questions.

Affective questions. There will always be conflicts in human interactions and relationships. It's how we deal with those conflicts that matters. And, most important, it's how we repair the relationships that exist between humans so that we can all get back to learning. This repairing process begins with meeting with the parties separately in order for them to speak freely, and for you to determine whether they are ready to meet with the others. We have found the following questions, developed by Costello and colleagues (2009), to be particularly helpful in getting students to talk about what happened. For the person with the challenging behavior, we might ask

- What happened?
- What were you thinking of at the time?
- What have you thought about since?
- Who has been affected by what you have done? In what way have they been affected?
- What do you think you might need to do to make things right? (p. 16)

For the person affected by the challenging behavior, we might ask:
- What did you think when you realized what had happened?
- What impact has this incident had on you and others?
- What has been the hardest thing for you?
- What do you think needs to happen to make things right? (p. 16).

Impromptu meetings. Engaging people with these affective questions will inevitably lead to a request for a meeting. We've seen this time and again. For example, when 4th grader Jacob was bullying 2nd grader Martin and realized the impact this was having on learning and the feeling of safety, Jacob asked for an impromptu conversation to attempt to repair the harm done. Importantly, all of the people who attend this type of meeting need to agree to be there. If the perpetrator is forced to be there, it is unlikely that he or she will learn from the experience or change as a result of it. If the victim is forced to be there, he or she might feel further victimized or scared and will not be prepared to accept the apology or advocate for what he or she thinks should be done about it. If the bystanders are forced to be there, they may not commit to the process and might mock the whole event, telling their peers what a waste of time the meeting was. Assuming that all of the members of the impromptu conference agree to be there, a facilitator typically leads the session and structures the conversation. Although there may be times that the facilitator steps out of the room, the resolution meeting is not a free-for-all or a laundry list of complaints lodged against the perpetrator. Rather, it is a structured conversation focused on the incident at hand in which each person gets to have his or her say, with the goal of repairing the relationships and providing a learning opportunity for everyone involved.

Circles. The conversations that students have in restorative practices are based on trust and expectations. This develops with low-stakes conversations that occur regularly in classrooms. There are all kinds of circle conversations that students can have: something that makes you really happy, something that you are worried about, something that you're thinking of doing on Friday night. These circles build students' habits at sharing their thinking publicly with their peers.

For example, Heather Anderson's 10th grade students regularly have circle meetings to check in with their teacher. One day, they were talking about an upcoming project that was to identify a worthy cause, one worth fighting for, and to develop a Facebook page for that cause. During their circle at the end of that class period, Ms. Anderson asked students to share their worthy cause and why they selected it. She started this circle by saying that she would be developing her cause page about pancreatic cancer because her aunt had been diagnosed with this a few weeks before. She broke into tears and thanked her students for listening and supporting her cause. As they went around the room, students shared their causes, some of which were emotional and some of which were not. Some examples included:

Roel: My cause is wildlife conservation because I think that too many animals are being killed and going extinct. It bothers me that we aren't doing more about this.

Adrianna: I'm thinking that I'll do mental health issues for teenagers because I've struggled with this personally. You all know that, and you really helped me, but I think it's time that I talked about this more openly. Yeah, that's what I think I'll do.

Ahmed: I am doing Islamaphobia (I think I made up that word) because many people fear Muslims and I want to be part of the education about this.

Carla: I am [pause]. I think I'll do [pause]. It's about gangs. It's because my dad leaves every night to be in his gang. He's high up now, but I don't know if he will come home at night. [crying] I don't know what he does, but gangs are bad. They're ruining my life. [handed the tissue box from a peer]

These circle conversations prepare students for the harder conversations they will have, either whole class or small group, when harm is done. They learn to advocate for themselves, they learn to reflect on their actions and whether their actions harm others, and they learn to internalize standards of behavior that are consistent with *do not harm*. That's not to say that problems don't erupt in schools that use restorative practices; they do. It is to say that the reactions to these eruptions provide students an opportunity to learn and grow as a result. We have only scratched the surface of the work that needs to be done to really build a restorative practices–based school. For more information, please visit www.iirp.org.

Organizational Principles

As with the other pillars, there are a number of organizational principles that can be effective in creating a school culture that values the principles of *do no harm*. To facilitate your work on this pillar, we provide the principles we have found effective. Of course, each school will need to customize this list and develop principles that guide their work.

1. *Rules don't teach behavior. People do.*

2. *Teach students about the dimensions of doing no harm—to self, to others, and to the environment. Use these as cognitive tools to review behavioral choices and infractions with students.*

3. *Foster a level of responsible trust between student and staff so students know there are adults they can go to when school and life seems overwhelming. Share time and space together.*

4. *Foster self-regulation to build the capacity of students to function at school each day.*

5. *Invest in a preventative mindset that seeks to address potential difficulties before they spin into crisis.*

6. *Learn and deploy restorative practices.*

Although these seem quite simple, in truth they are not. The temptation to react and punish is a strong one, and all of us are in danger of reverting back to a culture where behavior is managed rather than developed. We are all vulnerable to particular conditions that push our buttons and want to make us retaliate. Service cycles are especially important for making decisions and determining a course of action. Administrators and teachers rarely enjoy the luxury of discussing the difficulties a student is having in school, and these service cycles build the collective confidence of everyone in the building that decisions are equitable and responsive to all.

Putting Principles into Action with Service Cycles

Because a culture of doing no harm should be first and foremost a proactive one, the first two learning cycles adopt a preventative approach. However, problems do arise in all schools, and figuring out how to respond can be challenging in the heat of the moment. The final two cycles describe a problem-solving approach for restoring the school culture when it has been disrupted.

Proactive classroom environment for learning. People's attention and appetite for distraction fluctuate throughout the day. Levels of alertness and fatigue vary as well, and they are rarely synchronized with everyone else in the room. This is true whether you are 5 or 55. A classroom of students will experience an ebb and flow of physical, cognitive, and psychological energy during each lesson. It is truly an exercise in futility to build a system that presumes that attention and alertness will remain uniformly high. Wise teachers structure their classrooms to accommodate these vacillations. This first service cycle (see below) requires that the learning environment is structured to reduce the likelihood that disruptions will occur.

- Understandable routines and procedures are taught and revisited.
- Students have opportunities to interact with each other.
- Teachers and the students need periodic escapes from learning, such as a self-initiated break, the ability to choose a task, and even some hallway TLC.
- Students help each other.

Jeannie Arlington makes sure that her 3rd graders know and use the helping curriculum in her classroom. The entire school uses this service cycle beginning in kindergarten. Called the helping curriculum, this work was inspired by Sapon-Shevin's (1998) recommendation that all children and adults need to know how to

- Ask for help when it's needed.
- Offer help to another when they see someone struggling.
- Accept help when it's offered.
- Politely decline help when a person wants to try it for a bit longer.

"It has helped me to remember there's not just one teacher in the classroom; there's 31 of us here," she said. "My job is to figure out how they can build a helping culture right here in this room." She makes sure that materials are in easy reach of students so that they can access supplies when needed. They use role-playing to examine situations when a person might say, "Thank you, but not right now. I'm going to try this again first." Importantly, before beginning a small-group task, she alerts them to signs that their peers may need assistance. "By making sure to teach about the helping curriculum regularly, I head off lots of potential problems that might otherwise occur. And they really get to see that everyone has something to offer, even if it's just a kind word of encouragement," Ms. Arlington said.

Hallway TLC. As described previously, the practice of having informally staffed areas expressly for the purpose of offering a listening ear has been a foundational shift in our school's practice. It was borne out of a move to a larger facility where it was more difficult to observe student movement. Within weeks, we had developed a service cycle for making it a signature feature of the school. It was important to invite any caring adult to sit there. The only qualification needed is to be a good listener. It has also helped to reduce teacher anxiety when a student has been gone for a while from the classroom. A glance down the hallway confirms whether a student is in the Hallway TLC area.

- Staff training about what it is and isn't.
- Selecting locations.
- Decisions about who will use it.
- An open invitation: "How can I help you? I have the time."
- Referring students for more extensive supports.

Analyze the causes of the behavior. A fundamental shortcoming with some school discipline procedures is the cookbook approach: Match infraction A to punishment B, stir, then bake as directed. The problem is, as Bandura taught us, that motivation plays a key role in understanding behavior. It is simply not enough to take a cookie-cutter approach to outward signs of behavior. Humans are just too complicated for that to work. We agree that certain violations require a formulated response that is procedurally sound. But we worry when many of the garden-variety misbehaviors of the school day are addressed in the same lockstep manner as more serious infractions. Didn't come to class with a pencil? Zero points for today—it says so right in the syllabus. Late for class? Lockout. It says so right in the student handbook you signed in September. To be sure, this approach makes the job of the person who is sentencing the student easier, because all he or she needs to do is match A to B. But it doesn't address the underlying causes for the misbehavior in the first place, and it will not reduce the likelihood it will be repeated.

It's helpful to consider the communicative intent of the behavior—what is the person trying to say by doing or not doing something? At its most basic level, everything any of us do is for one of two things:

- Avoiding something
- Obtaining something

The student who comes to class without a pencil may be (1) avoiding classroom work; (2) avoiding asking his father, who was recently laid off from work, for 50 cents to buy a pencil from the school store; (3) seeking the attention of the teacher to be noticed because no one has acknowledged him since he arrived that morning; or (4) seeking the approval of his peers who are watching him get kicked out of class. It's hard to determine the most effective response to this situation without digging a bit deeper first. If he's seeking to avoid classroom work, sending him to the office works out nicely for him. But if he needs two quarters and some encouraging words, then scolding him isn't going to help the situation and will probably harm it. Presume that there's an underlying story, and have a conversation to figure out what it is. It may seem time-consuming, but consider how doing so can prevent future misbehavior. In order to informally analyze causes, and not just the behavior itself, consider the following service cycle:

- Build the staff's capacity to look for clues about motivation, not just the outward behavior.
- Take the time to have conversations with students about their problem behavior.
- Look at patterns of misbehavior across students and environments.
- Follow up with restorative practices as warranted.
- Establish procedures for students and teachers to easily resolve minor problems.

Young children aren't always able to articulate their own motivations (and neither are older students, come to think of it). But ferreting out the underlying story can guide effective decision making. Sarai Patel, a 1st grade teacher, knows that finding out the story behind the story can lead to quicker solutions. "It's not uncommon for me to experience a lot of tattling going on at this age," she said. "But there are a couple of kids who seem to do the lion's share of the tattling in this class. At first I attributed it to personality, but I started to realize there was more to it that that." Ms. Patel continued, "I talked to each one separately about tattling and discovered they had two very different reasons for it. I discovered that the Rebecca really wanted my attention. She liked the fact that we had these private conversations. I'm making a point to talk with her every morning about other things.

"But Chuy was a different story," she said. "It made him anxious when he saw violations. I realized that he didn't have the same sense of security as others. I talked to the guidance counselor, and she told me that his home life is pretty unstable right now. The family has had a rough time with finding a long-term housing arrangement," Ms. Patel said. "I'm working to make sure that I'm spending a few moments several times a day checking in with him. I assure him when we're going to be doing something new. It seems to be helping, too. With both kids I'm listening to a bit less tattling. Maybe because I'm getting better at listening to them."

Restorative practices. Despite our best efforts to prevent problems from occurring, they still do. Having a system of restorative practices in place means that the collective efforts of the school are focused on resetting the school community when one or more of its members have been harmed. We believe that this practice needs to be institutionalized, and not just used occasionally by a few people, for it to truly impact the school community. The work of restorative practices requires building expertise across the school campus so that everyone can play a part in this effort. Not all staff members need to be facilitators. Many schools select a team to receive additional professional development in restorative practice and draft the school's restorative service cycle. Their expertise and experience adds to the effectiveness of each restorative conversation. A suggested service cycle for restorative practices includes:

- Build staff and student awareness of restorative practices philosophy and procedures.
- Establish restorative practices procedures for meeting individually and separately with each party.
- Bring the parties together when they are ready for a restorative practices session.
- Follow up with involved parties so they are aware of the status of the incident.

- Foster communication in classrooms with restorative practices principles in place.

Sixth grade math teacher Bobby Diaz uses circles at least once a week to discuss math-related, and sometimes life-related, issues. "I start circles the first week of school, and I tell them about the importance of the circle in mathematics. Our first circle of the year is always about their math fears. We pass a small wooden abacus around—that's our talking stick—so that only one person can talk at a time. They'll talk about being called up to the board to work out a problem, or having their mind go blank just before a test," he said.

Sometimes the topics are about the issues that concern 12-year-olds. "One circle we did a few weeks ago was called, 'If you knew me, you'd know...,'" he said. Some of their responses were funny, like the one boy who said, 'If you knew me, you'd know that I have the stinkiest feet in my whole family!' We all laughed about that. But then another boy said, 'If you knew me, you'd know that I have diabetes and I have to give myself a shot every day.' I already knew this, of course, but until that day he had never told any of his classmates." Mr. Diaz paused for a moment. "I was really proud of him and of the supportive reaction that he got from the other kids. He was so afraid that having a chronic illness would make him different and weird. I'm glad he's beginning to realize that it's just part of who he is, but it doesn't define him."

Action Research Tools

Once again, we encourage you to take a good *look* at whether the culture you are developing in your school promotes the tenets of *do no harm*. We offer you some tools to organize this analysis. As you collect information and consider your observations, *think* about the types of principles that might be adopted, the types of service systems that might be more purposefully thought out, and the sorts of norms that are currently unproductive in building this pillar of your school's culture. And then, provide leadership, engage your staff, decide on focused actions, and choose to act in a way that is likely to enhance this aspect of your cultural identity.

The way that students experience school may not be the way that they describe it to adults. In many cases, students do not believe that the adults can or will do anything about the harassing situations that they witness. As a result, students often indicate that things are fine at their school, until they are asked to respond to surveys anonymously. When students are provided an opportunity to share their true experiences and are invited to take time on the survey to respond honestly, they offer valuable data that can be used to create change. Action research tool 7 is a sample student survey that can be used to assess the culture as the students experience it.

Another way to assess the culture of the school is to audit the discipline records. What you are looking for is trends in the data that will allow you to take action to make the environment more conducive to learning. If there are significant disruptions in a given classroom, learning is being compromised. The action you take may or may not involve coaching for the teacher. There have been times when we thought that a teacher needed to focus on classroom management, and there are other times when we believed that the class needed other changes, such as increased rigor, routines for productive group work, or a clear message about expectations from an administrator. To determine which action is appropriate to take, a good starting point is the analysis of discipline data. We suggest looking at referrals, suspensions, and expulsions for trends. Are there grade levels or departments that more frequently discipline students using these tools? Are some students statistically more likely to be disciplined, such as African American males (as suggested in several research studies according to Townsend, 2000)? Are some times of day, or locations in the school, likely to generate more disciplinary actions? Action research tool 8 is a discipline audit useful in answering these questions. Please note that the ethnicity categories vary by location, and you should use the ones consistent with your state reporting.

A third action research tool that we have found useful relates to the teachers' perceptions of student behaviors, and if these behaviors are being addressed (see action research tool 9). We have found that this tool is useful as a processing guide for teachers, who sometimes just want a place to record their perspectives on the situation. When this information has been recorded, teachers know that they are being listened to and expect that action will follow. A careful analysis of this information will reveal areas of needed attention as well as areas of success. It is important that teachers be encouraged to be honest and that this information not be used against them when they openly discuss their perspectives on student behavior. If people think that there are consequences to their honesty, they will no longer be honest, and you will be faced with making decisions and taking action on inaccurate data. Of course, this analysis can yield information about professional development and coaching that needs to occur, but not evaluation comments or disciplinary actions.

Conclusion

A *do no harm* school culture requires a shift in how both students and staff perceive the maintenance of an orderly environment conducive to learning. The beliefs and traditions enculturated in each of them can yield strong feelings that may run counter to the one you are trying to create at school. Creating a culture that restores trust and teaches effective behavior and choice requires a schoolwide commitment and ongoing professional and student development. The boy who says, "My old man told me never to start a fight but always finish one," must reconcile both his home and school traditions. He needs lots of support in figuring out how to do so. In addition, a teacher who wants to know how many days of suspension you doled out for a classroom infraction may have come from a school culture where an administrator handled all the behavior problems. She needs support in understanding that all of us have a role in creating a culture where taking care of ourselves, others, and this place is how we measure our actions and reactions.

CHAPTER 4

Choice Words

Maria, on the day of her *quinceañera*, stands in front of the mirror, looking at her petite five-foot frame in a bright white chiffon dress. Perhaps she was wondering if this would be the day she would finally feel comfortable taking off that mischievous little girl mask she had been hiding behind and celebrate her coming of age. Perhaps this was the day her family and friends would give her the confidence to stand as a proud young woman. Perhaps today she could let down the guard she had been using to shield the years of psychological and physical reminders that she was a weak and powerless failure. Perhaps today, she thought. Surely the day was filled with ceremony, well wishes, worldly advice, and a big celebration full of food, song, dance, and laughs.

Yet, despite the joy of an event she had been anticipating for most of her life, it was a casual statement from her uncle that ended up defining the day. His words threw her far back into the shell she hoped to have emerged out of that day. Two months later, when she confided to one of her teachers, she repeated her uncle's words, said to her as she entered the backyard party: "You're getting a little plump." Surely the uncle was trying to be sarcastic, a little innocent humor as Maria was barely 125 pounds. Or perhaps he was awkward in commenting on the fact that puberty was changing this petite girl's body into that of a young woman. Regardless, that statement defined

Maria's quinceañera, and in the two months that followed, she had barely eaten a thing. What she did eat, she threw up. As she sat before us, she had dropped to 107 pounds and claimed she had no interest in food at all.

Apparently, what she decided she could control was her weight. She would not be that plump thing her uncle caused her to see every time she looked in the mirror. She rebelled at the thought of the doctors getting involved to make her eat. She was so close to getting to the 100-pound weight she thought would make her life whole. Until then, this fragile and frail girl, whose hair was beginning to fall out, and who was skin and bones, looked in the mirror and saw a plump, powerless little girl she wanted nothing to do with.

We certainly are not psychiatrists or medical doctors, and we cannot begin to tell you how an anorexic girl can actually look in the mirror and see a person who has no resemblance to her actual physical self. We would argue that this tragic set of real events is also a metaphor for large numbers of students who have little idea who they are looking at when they look into their life's mirror. The lack of a positive self-image and self-concept among adolescents presents huge challenges for us. Without a positive self-image, many fundamental attributes that support learning and engagement such as confidence, trust, and passion will be lacking. We are not advocating for the EST workshops of the 1960s to replace the modern-day classroom or a relevant and rigorous curriculum. We believe understanding and building student self-confidence and image can occur concurrently with our instruction and must occur in all of our interactions with students.

The *Choice Words* Pillar

We named this pillar in tribute to Peter Johnston, who reminded us that our language affects children's learning. Although he is only one of many to say this (e.g., Denton, 2007), the examples he provided in his book (2004) have resulted in significant changes in teacher talk in classrooms around the world. Simply said, language "creates realities and invites identities" (p. 9), two things our students need. Choosing words carefully so that they build students' identities is an important aspect of building the culture of a school.

When the language students hear helps them tell a story about themselves that is one of possibility and potential, students perform in ways that are consistent with that belief. Alternatively, when students hear language that tells them that they can't do something, they perform that way. Of course, these are not instant reactions, but rather profiles that develop over many years. The essential question is this: is your school a place where students rediscover, develop, and use their talents, gifts, and natural capabilities? We could also ask, do teachers consciously develop students' self-concepts and the stories they tell about themselves? If not, that is, if students do not believe they are capable of great learning, of finding their passions, or of authorizing a recognized work of quality, they are unlikely to create a personal connection with their education, and they will be less likely to engage and learn. How do students begin to trust that the adults around them will put them in their element? How do they learn to look in the mirror and see a reader, a writer, or a beautiful and capable person? These messages must emanate from your school's culture and the belief in students and their learning.

The Stories We Tell About Ourselves

Each of us has a personal narrative, a story that we tell about ourselves. As Block (2008) notes, stories "are crucial to our knowing who we are; they provide a sense of identity" (p. 35). Riessman (1993) says, "Individuals become the autobiographical narratives by which they tell about the lives" (p. 2). Our story is formed by the interactions we have with other people and the internal dialogue we have with ourselves. The story may or may not be accurate, but it is our own and guides our dealings with the world. Importantly, not all stories we tell ourselves, and about ourselves, are positive. Block reminds us, "We need to distinguish between the stories that give meaning to our lives and help us find our voice, and those that limit our possibility" (p. 35).

We are reminded of a 3rd grader who reported, "I'm a good writer, but I don't do good in math." When asked how she knew this, she said that she "never did too good on the homework" and that her teacher used to tell her that she needed more practice. In reality, this student's test scores were not bad. She scored above the 50th percentile, but the story she was telling herself, and us, was limiting her possibility. Thankfully, these stories can be changed. According to Block,

> Limiting stories are the ones that present themselves as if they were true. Facts. Our stories of our own past are heartfelt and yet are fiction. All we know that is true is that we were born. We may know for sure who our parents, siblings, and other key players in our drama were. But our version of all of them, the meaning and memory that we narrate to all who will listen, is our creation. Made up. Fiction. And this is good news, for it means that a new story can be concocted any time we choose. (p. 35)

Another case in point. Mykelia was abused as a child. There is documentation of this fact, and she was removed from her family at age 8. The story she used to tell about her abuse related to her belief that she was a "bad girl who always got punished." In essence, she believed that to a certain extent she deserved the punishments. As a middle school student, she could articulate that she did not deserve to be physically abused, but she also concluded that she needed to be punished for the things that she did wrong. The story she told herself changed when she realized, with a lot of guidance and support from a social worker, that she was not responsible for her abuse. Yes, she had been a victim, but that did not define her.

We are not saying that bad things don't really happen to children and young adults. We have too many experiences to suggest otherwise. What we are saying is that the story they tell about themselves, the things that they come to believe about themselves, may or may not be true. Some of the stories may be limiting their potential, and we have the power to change that.

Where Do These Stories Come From?

The simple answer is: the stories we tell ourselves come from our interpretations of our experiences. These experiences are structured by our environment and the adults in it. This process starts very early and is, at least in part, structured by the differences in our parents' child rearing and interactions with us. For example, in an in-depth study of interactions between parents and their children, Lareau (2003) noticed patterns that led to the transmission of differential advantages to children. As she reports, "there was quite a bit more talking in middle-class homes than in working-class and poor homes, leading to the development of greater verbal ability, larger vocabularies, more comfort with authority figures, and more familiarity with abstract concepts" (p. 5). These benefits play out in the stories that children tell about themselves. Think about the child who has numerous experiences interacting with authority figures as an equal, such as being encouraged to ask questions of the doctor during an appointment or shaking hands and looking in the eye of the repair person coming to the house. This child begins to tell a story about competence and holds the idea that others value her opinions.

The stories that children tell about themselves do not develop solely from their interactions with parents. Teachers and other educational staff members have a profound impact on the identity development of young people (Denton, 2007; Johnston, 2004). After all, we do spend hours and hours with them for at least 180 days. In many cases, this is more interaction time than they have with their parents. In fact, some children have significantly more interactions with their teachers than with their parents. When teachers understand that the language they use can build the stories children tell about themselves, they use this knowledge to help students develop a positive identity. For example, imagine a classroom in which students are regularly asked, "Tell me more about that. I'm interested in your ideas." The message is clear: you have something worth talking about, and I care about what you have to say. We have observed a classroom in which this was the norm. The children, who were all 6 or 7, started out the year saying very little and often indicating that they had nothing to add. By December, the classroom was filled with talk. Student production, not just in terms of talk, but also in writing and other tasks, had dramatically increased. The students clearly had a different story to tell about themselves: they were important, and they had ideas. What was even more impressive was the ways in which students interacted with each other. They could be regularly observed asking peers for more information, thanking their peers for sharing, and communicating that other people were important.

As a note of caution, Johnston (2004) reminds us, "Students have to be convinced that our words are real and not empty flattery" (p. 38) if we want this approach to be effective. In other words, it's not enough to copy a series of statements from a book and say them to students. It's really about the beliefs each of us holds and how those beliefs are expressed through our interactions with others. These interactions build the community, the culture, of the classroom and the school. This requires a change in the conversations we have, moving from problems to possibilities and from fear and fault to gifts, generosity, and abundance (Block, 2008). Although conversations, language, and labels are critical to the development of stories, so are experiences. As educators, we plan a number of experiences for students. Later in this chapter we will focus on the interactions that students have with each other and how to build those experiences such that students tell stories about their worth to the group. But we are reminded of other experiences that students have, such as the one that allowed Araceli to change the story she told about herself.

At the time, Araceli was a 15-year-old 9th grader who could stand five feet tall on her tiptoes, but she would never dare stretch so high. She was content to never show initiative. Perhaps in that way she could go unnoticed and if she went unnoticed, perhaps nobody would know how unimpressive and insignificant she thought she was. She was compliant enough; she did what she was told; she completed her assignments and was no behavior problem. We imagine this responsive compliance also helped keep attention off her. It is quite possible when Araceli looked in the mirror, she had trouble identifying any image at all. What she did see, when asked, was a student who had failed 1st grade and would not attend college.

It happened that Araceli was unable to write much in her hospital internship fieldwork log because, as she put it, "they did not give me anything to do." As part of her school curriculum, internships had been arranged for all students, and Araceli was placed in a clinical setting, in part because she had no ideas about what she would do in her future. The problem was when she was asked if she *wanted* to do something specific, she would shyly say no and therefore was offered few experiences. She was encouraged by many school staff to step forward and say yes the next time she was offered the opportunity. She reluctantly agreed, mostly out of respect for an adult whom she trusted.

It happened that that particular week her hospital rotation was in labor and delivery. She was in with a patient who spoke only Spanish. The nurse knew only enough Spanish to get by, and the ob/gyn knew less. The patient was scared and alone and immediately picked up on the fact that Araceli was Latina and called her over to her bedside. She asked Araceli if she could speak Spanish, and when the girl told her she could, the woman asked if she would help her. Araceli, as promised, said yes. The patient grabbed Araceli's hand and started to cry. And there Araceli stood, all five feet of her, dressed in brown hospital scrubs, acting as the translator between the doctor and his patient. Unfortunately, the patient's status deteriorated, and the baby's wellbeing was in jeopardy. The doctor decided to perform a C-section. He asked Araceli if she wanted to scrub in and stay with the patient. Araceli remembered her commitment and said yes, if the patient wanted her to. The patient grabbed Araceli's hand, unwilling to let go. Araceli talked the patient through the entire procedure. She saw the doctor deliver the baby and heard the newborn cry out her first sounds. She stood back in awe of what she had just witnessed. The nurse leaned over and asked the mom if she had decided on a name. The mom told her without hesitation that she was naming the baby Araceli.

Who do you think Araceli saw in the mirror when she got home that night? How willing do you think she was then to begin trusting herself, seeing and celebrating her self-worth, ready to take bold steps toward her future? How willing do you think she was in allowing us to be her partners in that great journey? The story that Araceli started telling herself on that day changed dramatically. She graduated from high school, with an admission letter to a four-year university. She has a career goal, to become a nurse, and a plan to get there. Really, she is the same person. She just has a different story to tell, and that story provided her with possibilities.

The Power of Words

We are shaped by the language we use about ourselves, and by the language used by others about us. This reality requires us to be mindful of the language we use to provide direction and feedback and of the harmful nature of sarcastic comments, even if were just trying to be cute or funny. In other words, we have to consciously *choose our words,* as communication is a defining element of our school culture.

Language builds our identities, and in turn our identities are reflected in the language we use. Tracy (2002) talks about four dimensions of our identities:

- The *master identity* of gender, age, and ethnicity
- The *interactional identity* of roles such as daughter, brother, student, and teacher
- The *personal identity* of personality and character traits
- The *relational identity* during every conversation, such as whether the partners are equal or unequal, friendly or hostile, and so forth

A person brings all of these dimensions of identity to every exchange, and the first three are more fixed. However, the fourth, the relational identity, is created during every communication exchange. Whether we are in 1st grade or the teacher of the 1st grader, the relational identities of each can vary with each conversation. Consider two examples:

Teacher: I told you to sit down and be quiet.

Student: But I…

Teacher: It's time for math, and we are all waiting for you so we can start. You are disrespecting the whole group.

Student: Yes, ma'am.

Now a second version:

Teacher: I can see you're having a hard time sitting still. What's going on?

Student: I have lots of energy!

Teacher: I can see that, but now it's time for us to begin math. We all learn better when you're with us. Is there something we can do to help you?

Student: [wriggling enthusiastically one more time] No, I got it. Now I'm ready!

In each exchange, the outcome was the same—the child sat still. But the first conversation probably left the student thinking about being scolded. The second exchange preserved the child's self-concept and didn't rely on shame to get cooperation. Therefore, he was more likely to focus on the business of learning to add. The relatively fixed identities of gender, age, and roles remained the same in each example, but the relational identity was the variable. In the second, the teacher approached the conversation with a different perception of how her identities influenced the outcome.

Denton (2007) says there are three goals in the language we use as teachers: (1) help students develop self-control, (2) build community, and (3) foster academic skills and knowledge. One teacher was so intent on the first that she prevented the second and third goals from ever being realized. Of course, all students will need redirection. But while the first teacher relied on coercion, the second chose to make it about empowering the student. She noticed and named the behavior she saw and gave him a reason why the class needed him to align his behavior to the task. She then gave him a moment to get himself ready. The second teacher turned it into an opportunity for him to practice self-control, rather than moving directly to controlling the situation herself.

It may seem like a small thing and really not worthy of our attention. After all, there are more pressing matters that weigh on all of us each day in a school. But these small exchanges build up or tear down a culture moment by moment. The rapidly shifting relational identities that we bring to each conversation have the power to inspire or deflate. In addition, these small exchanges can serve as the triggers for problematic behavior later on. What if the first student hadn't glumly replied, "Yes, ma'am"? He could have turned over his desk in anger, which in turn would require the involvement of more people. And it wouldn't be surprising for the teacher to report, "I told him to sit down and get started on his math, and he refused." And there is some truth to that. But what can't be heard is the tone. So instead of a 6-year-old learning about addition, you've got an angry one with his arms crossed and a scowl on his face sitting outside your office.

Alisha Coleman-Kiner, principal at Booker T. Washington High School in Memphis, Tennessee, is proud of her school's graduation rates, which have increased from 55 percent a few years ago to nearly 82 percent. When asked about how this was accomplished, she replied, "I loved my children. I hired people who would love my children. And then I did my job" (Coleman-Kiner, 2011, p. 25). Deb Gustafson, principal at Ware Elementary in Fort Riley, Kansas, has shepherded her school from being the first one in her state to be in program improvement to a place where 80 percent of the students meet or exceed state standards in reading and math (Education Trust, 2011). She told the staff, "[I'll] never reprimand them for anything except speaking to children inappropriately," reminding them that "it's grown-ups...who are responsible for setting the tone of schools" (Chenoweth, 2010, p. 20). Perhaps both principals understood that the power of the language teachers use with students can mean the difference between a focus on achievement and a focus on simply maintaining order. As Goodman notes, we can't allow ourselves to "succumb to a system of coercion rather than one of education" (2011, p. 22).

Really, the choice is ours. Do we want to educate or coerce children? Do we want them to tell stories about their potential or their failures? Language develops the mindsets from which children make decisions. Language is the most powerful weapon we have in changing student achievement and thus deserves a pillar of its own.

Fixed and Growth Mindsets

Elite athletes and their coaches know the power of visualization in performance. They use it to mentally rehearse their ideal movements in order to summon the skills they'll need in a game situation. These images can be external or internal and include visual, kinesthetic, and auditory images. But negative images can interfere with performance, especially by encouraging the athlete to replay mental tapes of future failure.

Negative labels are the school's equivalent of negative visualization in sports. Certainly members of various ethnic, gender, and language groups have experienced the negative labels of stereotyping. A student may labor under the low expectations based on the poverty of her parents, or he may have an outward demeanor that causes others to label him as "lazy" or to remark that "he just doesn't care." Wherever they come from, negative labels serve to limit, and over time they become a part of the student's story about her- or himself.

Carol Dweck (2006) says that people's stories about themselves take the form of a mindset about the world. A fixed mindset is a belief that "your qualities are carved in stone" and thus require the person to continually have to prove their worthiness or give up altogether (p. 6). A growth mindset, on the other hand, "is based on the belief that your basic qualities are things you can cultivate through your efforts" (p. 7). This is the mindset necessary for achievement, as those who possess a growth mindset are more willing to confront problems, take risks, and persist.

Think for a moment about two middle school students sitting in a science classroom. They are tasked with learning about the influence of genetic traits on predicting reproduction outcomes in breeding. They have been using a Punnett square with monohybrid crosses like the shape of a seed. Tough stuff, but so far, so good. But now they need to do a dihybrid analysis of two independent variables—seed shape and flower color. The task just got a lot harder. One student has a fixed mindset, and the other a growth mindset. You don't need to perform a Punnett square calculation to predict the likelihood that one will give up more easily than the other.

An interesting effect of mindset is its influence on persistence. The student with the fixed mindset is likely to stay interested only if she is immediately successful. Dweck calls it "thriving on the sure thing" (p. 23). The reverse is true for those with a growth mindset, who report a similar level of enjoyment whether they were successful or not. They rise to and even seek out things that will challenge them. In her words, "it's not about immediate perfection. It's about learning something over time: confronting a challenge and making progress." In contrast, "people with a fixed mindset expect ability to show up on its own, before any learning takes place" (p. 24).

Isn't that what schools are supposed to be about? If students already knew what we were going to be teaching them, they wouldn't have any need for us in the first place. Learning is *always* about failure—as the old adage goes, we learn from our mistakes. We don't want failure to go on without end, as we know that will defeat even those with a strong growth mindset. But we do know that all learners go through a stage called productive failure (Kapur, 2008). This is the time when they try something out and it doesn't work. But for learners with a fixed mindset, the internal dialogue is self-defeating and they give up too soon. The students with the growth mindset say, "Well, that didn't work. I wonder what went wrong?" And with that, they try again. The *it's never too late to learn* pillar reinforces this mindset by replacing the idea of "I am a failure" with one of "I have more learning and work to do to show that I can do this stuff."

Language and a Mindset of Achievement

But students arrive at our classroom doors with mindsets firmly in place. How can we change that? You'll recall that identity is formed in part by the relationships that occur during each conversation we have with another person (Tracy, 2002). This is precisely the place where we have tremendous influence. A well-meaning teacher with a fixed mindset of intelligence tells students, "You're so smart! Look at this test score!" A growth mindset teacher says, "You worked really hard to get this. How did you do it?" Praise of fixed traits reinforces a fixed mindset. We would never say to a student, "You did so well because you're _____" (fill in the blank with any racial, ethnic, or gender group) because we would rightfully label that as a stereotype. However, a fixed mindset stereotypes in a different way, because it makes some assumptions about a person and then generalizes it across all occasions. "You did so well because you're smart in math," we say, without giving credit for the hard work and determination of the student. The message she's likely to take away from that exchange is "I better do just as well on the next math test."

As Dweck noted, students with a fixed mindset require that their beliefs about themselves must always be tested. Nancy got an email from a student in one of her high school classes that read:

> I have looked at my score for the class. Right now my grade is at a 96%. I was wondering if there was anything I can do (poster, brochure, etc.) that I can bring to you on Monday that can help bring my grade up to a 98%. I would really appreciate it. Please email me back if there is anything I can possibly do. Thank you.

The student who wrote is a wonderful member of the class and works hard. She is truly a delight. Nancy wrote back expressing her concern:

> Like all of your classes, the grade comes from competencies. So far, you have a 96% average on your competencies because one of them was scored at 92%. Of course you can take that competency over because it's never too late to learn. I'm interested in your motivation. Can we talk further about this?

The student's reply came back four minutes later:

> Am I smart enough? My sister got a 98% when she took your class.

Nancy met with the student the following day and talked with her about grades. The student has a sibling who is one year older at the same school and who has done quite well academically. There has always been lots of comparisons of the two from the time they were young and continuing throughout school. While she would like to say that one conversation was all it took, the fact is that changing a mindset is slow. Students need to be blanketed in the kind of language (and policies) that value hard work and persistence. Grades can magnify this mindset, and while grading can't and shouldn't be eliminated, grading policies do need to be aligned with our own growth mindset that we must possess as educators. After all, our policies and procedures are the language of the school organization. We will discuss grades further in chapter 5. For now, we'll focus on the language that affects learning.

How Language Affects Learning

As we have noted, we are indebted to Peter Johnston for his efforts to analyze language and the impact that it has on children's learning. When his book, *Choice Words* (2004), was first published, we read it as part of an all-staff book study at the school where we worked. We committed to change our language and have seen amazing outcomes as a result. The impact that this has had on us, our students, and countless students around the world led us to name this pillar in Johnston's honor. His analysis includes a number of categories that are beyond the scope of this book, and we hope that you will take the time to read his work to continue your learning about this topic. For now, we will focus on four concepts that have significant potential to change the stories that students tell about themselves.

Attribute accomplishments to the student. When we interact with students and recognize their efforts, we should ask ourselves if they are doing work for us, to be compliant or to please us. As Johnston notes, some statements of praise position "the child in a subordinate position with respect to the teacher, the source of praise. It also subtly removes some of the responsibility for the accomplishment and gives it to the teacher" (p. 25). If we think about how we can phrase things so that the students understand their role in the accomplishment, they will begin to see that their efforts, and their strategic actions, allow them to meet their goals. In doing so, we can guide students to "attend to their internal feelings of pride" (p. 25), which will build their internal motivation, thus reducing their reliance on external motivation. The quotes that follow demonstrate ways to ensure that the accomplishments are attributed to the student:

- "I like the way you figured that out" (p. 5) offers the student a chance to integrate success into his or her story, even if the teacher guided the student's understanding. In addition, this statement says to the student, "You are one to figure things out," which in turn increases the likelihood that the student will persevere next time. In other words, it's building the growth mindset.
- "Kevin, your group told me that you were really helpful in explaining the meaning of this passage" does several things. First, it's not about pleasing the teacher, but rather acknowledging the assistance Kevin provided to peers. It also communicates that Kevin knows something and can explain things, increasing the likelihood that Kevin will try those things again. And finally, it recognizes that Kevin is a valued member of the community and his behavior is appreciated.
- "I bet you are proud of yourself" (p. 25) provides students an opportunity to reflect and realize that they are proud of what they have accomplished. It's very different from the more common statement made to students, "I am proud of you," which is really about pleasing the teacher. When we invite students to think about the fact that they

are proud of their accomplishments, they develop increased internal motivation and begin to tell a different story about their experiences.

Identity. Identity formation is the development of a unique personality, with individual beliefs and values that are formed by the interactions we have with others. This identity develops in stages across our lifespan and involves an understanding of the continuity of self, the uniqueness of self from others, and a sense of affiliations with others (Erikson, 1968; Kohlberg, 1981). The school system is responsible for students during a time of significant identity development, including moral development, competence, and fidelity. As we saw from the discussion on mindset, the things that adults say can facilitate student identity and personality, including their perseverance. Johnston (2004) notes that "building an identity means coming to see in ourselves the characteristics of particular categories (and roles) of people and developing a sense of what it feels like to be that sort of person and belong in certain social spaces" (p. 23). Consider the following quotes and their impact on identity:

- "What are you doing as a scientist today?" This question invites students to try on the role of scientist and think about what it means to do science work. There is the clear assumption that the student understands what scientists do and has made the choice to assume that identity, even if only temporarily.
- "James Patterson, a well-published author that I like to read, does the same kind of thing as you did. It's like a roller coaster ride until you get to the end and figure out who did it." This statement, made to a novice writer in a high school English class, suggested to him that he was a writer and that he engaged in writerly behaviors. If his identity was not yet that of a writer, this comment could very well be the one to start him on that journey.
- "You see the beauty in numbers" was said to a student who had the wrong answer, but who had worked hard to figure out the solution. Although the teacher also helped her get to the correct answer, the identity comment about seeing beauty in numbers was not lost on Danielle. Within days, she started talking about numbers being everywhere,

and she even started completing the practice work that would eventually help her performance and her grade.

Agency. Individuals with a strong sense of agency understand that their actions and the resulting accomplishments are linked. That does not mean that a person with a well-developed agency thinks that their efforts will always be fruitful, but rather that "if they act, and act strategically, they can accomplish their goals" (Johnston, 2004, p. 29). Bandura, who we focused on relative to self-concept in chapter 3, suggests that "to be an agent is to intentionally make things happen by one's actions… the core features of agency enable people to play a part in their self development, adaptation, and self renewal with changing times" (2001, p. 2). Students who decide they do not have agency do not engage in their learning, establish minimal goals for themselves, and choose easy tasks to complete. Students who decide that they do have agency increase their efforts, generate a lot of ideas, participate in conversations and group activities, and hold themselves to high standards. Again, as teachers, we have the power to develop students' agency. To do so requires that we help children "build bridges between action and consequence that develop their sense of agency" (Johnston, 2004, p. 30). The following quotes do just that:

- "How might you figure that out?" was asked of a group of 2nd graders who were trying to understand if the person they had selected to study for their project was still alive. They asked their teacher, who did not directly answer. Instead, she communicated with them that their efforts could result in their goal attainment, which in this case was access to information.
- "What will you do next?" provides the student with the clear message that there is something to do next and they, the students, have the power to do it. It also suggests that the teacher believes that the student knows what to do next and that the student is strategically evaluating the options. As with the other statements we make to build agency and identity, the teacher does not simply tell the student what to do. The student has responsibility, and the teacher assumes competence.

- "Why?" questions help students develop their understanding of the processes and procedures they use to accomplish things. As Johnston (2004) pointed out, "Asking why children do or say the things they do helps them develop the consciousness and hence ownership of their choices" (p. 37). We ask students why, or how did you know, or how did you figure that out, all of the time so that they verbalize their cognitive processes. If they rehearse it out loud, they are likely to do it again.

The damaging "but" and the power of "if." When teachers use "but" after a note of praise, they effectively discount the recognition, even if that recognition was consistent with the idea that the accomplishment was attributed to the student. For example, when the teacher says, "I see that you really worked on this problem, but you made a mistake in step 2," the student will focus on the error and not the acknowledgment of the effort. In this case, the growth mindset is probably not in operation because the student has really missed it and instead paid attention to the criticism. Similarly, when the teacher says, "Your group produced an interesting report, but I'm seeing a lot of off-task behavior," the students feel like they are in trouble and that their success with the product is not that important, overall.

In many cases, the "but" can be replaced with "and" with a very positive effect. In the first example, consider the difference an "and" makes: "I see that you're really worked on this problem, and you made a mistake in step 2." The effort is not discounted, and the student knows that she needs to attend to step 2. In other cases, the sentences need to be separated and perhaps rephrased. In our second example, the teacher could have said, 'Your group produced an interesting report. I am a little troubled by what I thought was some off-task behavior. Can you tell me about your problem-solving processes?" In this case, the students know that their efforts were successful and are invited to talk about their problem solving. Maybe they were off-task and will now have an opportunity to reflect on that. Maybe they weren't off-task and can explain that to the teacher.

The power of "if" in a statement to students often conveys choice and represents the transfer of power from the teacher to the student. There is a difference between saying to a student, "You need to edit this. This paragraph belongs here," and "If you were to rearrange these ideas, it might help the reader understand your perspective more quickly." There is a choice, and this approach provides the student with an opportunity to consider the impact of that choice, in this case, on readers. When teachers use these types of statements, including "if," as appropriate, students develop their sense of self and agency, which is very motivating and engaging.

The Power of the Teacher

In classrooms where students are collaborators and their experiences are valued and valid, they grow into thinkers and productive members of the community. As Block reminds us, "people will be accountable and committed to what they have a hand in creating" (2008, p. 24). If we want students to be accountable and committed to their classroom, and by extension their learning, they have to have a hand in creating the environment, which includes the interactions that occur in that environment.

As a foundational pillar, *choice words* requires that students be active participants in classroom conversations, and not just conversations with their teacher. They need to talk with one another, in significant ways, as they complete meaningful tasks. We have established a goal that 50 percent of the instructional minutes are devoted to student-to-student interaction and productive group work. While we don't always reach this goal on a daily basis, it is something we strive for because it provides students with many opportunities to "play an active role in the ownership and construction of knowledge" (Johnston, 2004, p. 54). It also provides the teacher with numerous opportunities to meet with individual students and small groups of students to guide their thinking. In doing so, we can build students' identity and agency through our interactions with them. Although it is beyond the scope of this book to provide detailed information about the implementation of productive group work, there are a number of resources available for people who want to continue their learning in this area, including these:

- *Productive Group Work: How to Engage Students, Build Teamwork, and Promote Understanding* (Frey, Fisher, & Everlove, 2009, ASCD)

- *Practice with Purpose: Literacy Work Stations for Grades 3–6* (Diller, 2005, Stenhouse)
- *Kagan Cooperative Learning* (Kagan, 1994, Kagan Cooperative Learning)

To reach this goal, students have to be taught how to talk with one another. This means that students need to develop the language of argumentation if they are going to be productive with their peers. We have found it very useful to provide students with sentence frames that they can use in their interactions with peers. For example, figure 4.1 contains a number of language frames, organized around science argumentation, that were used to teach students how to have conversations with one another. It does no good to invite students to take ownership of the conversations in the classroom if they have no experience doing this, or if they lack the language skills to engage. We introduce these types of frames as a scaffold for students, knowing that they will use them temporarily as they internalize the types of interactions they want to have with each other. As such, these frames provide students with an identity, that of one who asks and answers questions and is not afraid to agree and disagree, knowing that peers will treat each other with respect.

Organizational Principles

The language that we use with students about themselves and their learning is challenging to affect because most of it is there for a moment, and then gone. There is usually no evidence of it beyond the observed demeanor of the students. But listen for the stories students tell about themselves through their words and actions. And listen to the language of ordinary exchanges in and out of classrooms, as well as discussions in places away from students, like the teachers' lounge and office. These can be revealing in understanding the mindsets of the adults in the school. These organizational principles are the ones we use, and as with all the other organizational principles offered in this book, you will want to customize the list to include your school's improvement efforts.

FIGURE 4.1

Language Frames for Argumentation in Science

Making a claim	I observed _____ when _____. I compared _____ and _____. I noticed _____, when _____. The effect of _____ on _____ is _____.
Providing evidence	The evidence I use to support _____ is _____. I believe _____ (statement) because _____ (justification). I know that _____ is _____ because _____. Based on _____, I think _____. Based upon _____, my hypothesis is _____.
Asking for evidence	I have a question about _____. Does _____ have more _____? What causes _____ to _____? Can you show me where you found the information about _____?
Offering a counterclaim	I disagree _____ because _____. The reason I believe _____ is _____. The facts that support my idea are _____. In my opinion _____. One difference between my idea and yours is _____.
Inviting speculation	I wonder what would happen if _____. I have a question about _____. Let's find out how we can test these samples for _____. We want to test _____ to find out if _____. If I change _____, (variable in experiment) then I think _____ will happen, because _____. I wonder why _____? What caused _____? How would this be different if _____? What do you think will happen if _____ next?
Reaching consensus	I agree _____ because _____. How would this be different if _____? We all have the same idea about _____.

Source: Ross, D., Frey, N., & Fisher, D. (2009). The art of argumentation. *Science & Children, 47*(3), 28–31. Used with permission.

1. *The language we use can positively or negatively affect the learning of students. It's up to us to choose our words wisely.*
2. *We foster a growth mindset daily to unlock human potential.*
3. *We are builders of identity and agency.*
4. *The damaging "but" and the power of "if" are communicated in all of our exchanges.*
5. *We are eliminating sarcasm as a means of providing feedback or trying to be funny.*
6. *We provide extensive opportunities each day for students to experience the power of their words to shape their learning and the learning of others.*
7. *We listen.*

These principles collectively communicate our values as communicators. In the same way that we teach our students about the language skills they will need for a successful professional and personal life, we must also continue to teach ourselves. The service cycles for the *choice words* pillar are our way of articulating the lessons about the power of language.

Putting Principles into Action with Service Cycles

The service cycles represent the routines that we use to ensure that the adults in the school use language across settings and circumstances that positively influences the stories children tell to and about themselves. As the principles imply, *choice words* is a construct that requires close monitoring and frequent practice in order to significantly shape the tone of the school. Therefore, these service cycles are designed to address locations and circumstances beyond teacher-led instruction.

Deescalating behavior. Problematic behavior is never static—it is always in flux as it rapidly rises and falls. But in too many cases we have witnessed (and sometimes been party to) an adult's response that escalated the problematic behavior. Doug and Nancy saw this in a science classroom in a high school they were visiting. When the teacher asked the class a question, one boy responded with a mildly humorous remark that elicited some chuckles from the class. But this enraged the teacher, who took this as a sign of disrespect. The teacher moved farther away, to the other side of the room, in fact, and then chastised the boy in front of the class. "I will *not* tolerate that in my classroom," he shouted. "And while you're at it, you need to take your hat off *right now*!"

Doug and Nancy looked at each other. The hat? What did that have to do with anything? And why had the teacher moved at least 10 feet away from the student before addressing him? That's when we noticed a security supervisor, a very large man, who moved closer to the student as the teacher scolded him. You would think that we would have noticed him before, but we hadn't. Faced with the public dressing down in front of his peers, an order that had seemed arbitrary under the circumstances, and a large man moving toward him in an aggressive manner, the student did what most reasonable people would do: he fled.

Doug followed him out the door, only to see him being stopped by another security supervisor and an assistant principal. They began barking orders at the boy and physically steered him to the office. Doug called the principal, a friend of ours, on his cell phone, to explain what had occurred in the classroom and what seemed to be transpiring now. The principal met us in the hallway outside class, and we informed him of what we saw. That's when we learned that the teacher had a security person in his room because he had so many problems with negative student behaviors. The principal met with the student and deescalated the situation. Within minutes, the boy's demeanor changed from arms folded tightly and eyes shifting back and forth, to one that appeared more relaxed. He was leaning forward, making eye contact with the principal, and speaking in a calm voice.

Keep in mind what started all of this: a silly but harmless answer to a teacher's question. Everything else was an escalation on the part of the adults. We don't hold the student blameless, but it is essential to recognize that even small transgressions can devolve into major incidences in the wrong hands.

It's the responsibility of every adult to deescalate problematic behaviors whenever possible. Here is a service cycle much like the one used that day:

- Speak quietly to the student in a calm voice.
- Keep your body language open and relaxed.

- Remove the student from the environment if it appears to be agitating the student further.
- Listen to the student's side of the story and resist interrupting.
- Move to restoring the student back to a learning condition as soon as possible.
- Follow up with other involved parties.

Your district or state department of education will have further detailed support materials and professional development for deescalating students. As you review these resources, consider building this service cycle to include additional techniques.

Do the next right thing. They say that a journey of a thousand miles begins with a single step, but in truth, most of us can get overwhelmed with the size of a task. Paralysis sets in at the thought of the enormity or complexity of the problem that needs to be resolved. In fact, these roadblocks to forward progress can cause many of us to remain fixed in a place as we try to determine what we should do next. This service cycle has been invaluable to us in working with adults and students as we help them with their decision making. We have adopted the language of active listening and advising by asking people to "do the next right thing." Our intent is to offer people a doorway to resolving their problems, rather than simply directing them as to what should happen. Additionally, it helps us to move a conversation forward when it has become stuck in the language of complaint, worry, or self-pity. Here is the service cycle we use for helping others to begin to solve a problem or approach a complex task:

- Listen to the description of the problem or task.
- Ask clarifying questions to assist the person in differentiating between the central problem or task and issues that are distracting them from beginning.
- Restate the problem or task as you understand it.
- Ask them what the *next* right thing to do would be.
- Write down their ideas for them.
- If they are stuck, offer some ideas for how to begin.

- Make a plan to follow up with the person to see if he or she put the plan into action.

We have found the "next right thing to do" language to help a student mediate a behavioral conflict as well as initiate an academic recovery plan. Children and adolescents commonly would like for problems or tasks to be completely resolved in one step. When they can't figure out what that one step might be, they remain frozen, unable to act. For example, Will, a 7th grade student, has fallen behind in his assignments for his English class, and he has been ducking his teacher's inquiries about when she might expect them. His parents have been checking his grades at home using the school's web-based student information system, and now they are asking the same questions.

Will confided in his math teacher from last year, a trusted adult in his life. Mr. Anzalone listened to Will's mixture of fretting and anger at his English teacher and parents for "hassling me so much." "I wish they'd get off my case and leave me alone!" Will said. "It sounds to me like the real problem is that you've got these assignments overdue and you're not sure where to begin," said Mr. Anzalone. "But if you could get caught up, all the other stuff would go away."

"But I don't know what I should do first! I've got this persuasive essay on mandatory voting to do, plus there's all these vocabulary assignments. And then I have to do this dumb presentation on folktales of America," Will whined.

"OK, I can hear how overwhelmed you're feeling. And you can't just do one thing and then it's all magically taken care of. You've gotten yourself into a hole by making a series of poor decisions. So let's think about it together— what would the next right thing be to do?" asked the teacher.

"Well, I guess I could do the essay first," Will said reluctantly.

"Hmm, that sounds like an important step, but a pretty big one. Let's back it up a little further. Where could you start?" Mr. Anzalone probed further.

For the next several minutes, the two talked as the teacher made a list of things that would need to occur. Mr. Anzalone then offered, "You've got the start of a plan here, but you need help in prioritizing it. It seems to me that you need to meet with your English teacher next. That might be the next right thing to do, so that she can see that you're paying attention to this and taking responsibility."

"I guess you're right," said Will as he took the list. "But at least I can tell her I talked with you about it."

"It sounds to me like you already did the next right thing by telling me what was troubling you," Mr. Anzalone said. "You've got lots of people in your court, like your teachers and especially your parents. You're not going to make this right by doing one thing. But if you keep asking yourself, what's the *next* right thing to do, it will help you put one foot in front of the other," he said.

"Yeah, you're right," Will grinned. "And after I talk to Ms. Halperin, I need to tell my parents what my plan is. That will be the next 'next right thing to do.'"

"Sounds like a plan," Mr. Anzalone said as the bell rang for the next period. "Let's talk again tomorrow and you can tell me how it went."

The importance of compliments. All of us need recognition for our accomplishments and efforts. The compliments we offer one another serve to maintain the relationships between humans. An unexpected compliment lifts the mood and can make your day. None of us are beyond the influence of a well-placed compliment. Without question, the language of offering compliments sets a tone for the ways we communicate when conversations are more difficult.

Of course, the compliments need to be authentic. An insincere one will do more damage than good, and the person delivering it will be regarded suspiciously: "If he lied about this, what else is he lying about?" As noted earlier, when teachers are talking with students about academic matters, we want to attribute the accomplishment to the student in order to foster a growth mindset. But it's also important to acknowledge the whole child, not just the student sitting in a science class. "I saw the PR [personal record] you posted yesterday at the track meet! There aren't many people who can run that fast. Congratulations!" lets the student know you take an interest in his life beyond his science learning. "That color looks great on you. It makes your eyes really pop!" lets the student know that you see her, not just her performance in math.

Students should also be taught to give and receive compliments so that they can experience the pleasures of both. In fact, Jack Canfield (2007) recommends this as part of the regular classroom experience. This can occur during a circle, as when 2nd grade teacher Brandy Lewis makes it a topic every Friday afternoon. "I start by reminding them about what a good compliment is, and each of us compliments the person to the right of them. That way I can make sure that everyone gets one. I ask them to think about the whole week and what they noticed," she said. Children say things like, "Hannah, your handwriting is so good!" or "I like the soccer shirt you're wearing today, Miles." Ms. Lewis observed, "It's a nice way for us to end the week before we go our separate ways," she said. "I want those compliments they hear to follow them home."

A suggested service cycle for giving compliments includes:

• Address the person by name.
• Name the accomplishment or attribute.
• Accept the compliment and say "thank you."
• [For older students] Back up your compliment with "because."
• Follow the compliment with a question to get a conversation going.
• Send a handwritten note home to the student, specifically complimenting student actions that deserve recognition. We call these "grit letters."

With older students, we add a few more steps. We ask them to give evidence using the word "because" ("You look really happy today because you're smiling a lot"). At times, we also ask them to add a question to begin a conversation, such as "I like the shoes you're wearing today. Are they as comfortable as they look?" Karina Petrov uses this method as a way of making sure that students stay in touch with one another in her 10th grade English class. "We do silent interviews every few weeks, and they pair with a different person each time," she said. "They start with separate papers and begin with writing a compliment with a 'because' and a question and then pass it to the other person," Ms. Petrov said. "They read what the other person wrote and then reply to it in writing. I give them a few minutes and they exchange papers like you would do for a spoken conversation. Then the students tell the rest of the class what they learned about their partner. I want them to keep doing this so that it becomes easier for them to show their interest in other people and to learn about others in a safe way. The kids make fun of this activity, but when I haven't done it for awhile, they'll say, 'Ms. P, when are we going to do silent interviews again?'"

Listening to students. We would be remiss in a chapter about the power of words to not also address the essential value of silence. The spaces we provide in a conversation allow the other speaker to clarify thoughts and elaborate on ideas. It's also when we demonstrate active listening. But this is more than "passively receiving someone's words. It's searching for the speaker's intended meaning" (Denton, 2007, p. 73). We're all guilty of using the time when we're not speaking for formulating what we will say next. But the problem with that is that you have likely missed the intended meaning because you were too busy listening to the voice in your own head. There are several compelling reasons for active listening:

- Listening lets us know the child.
- Listening builds a sense of community.
- Listening makes our questioning more effective.
- When we listen, students take their learning more seriously.
- Our listening helps students become better communicators. (Denton, 2007, p. 79)

Many of the qualities of active listening are embedded in previous service cycles, especially in regard to using body language to connote openness and paraphrasing to show that you are thinking about the speaker's message. The pauses that occur when the speaker is finished can carry the message that you are unhurried and attentive. In addition, students will often add more information when there is space to do so. This is sometimes called Wait Time II because it follows the student's initial answer. These pauses also invite other students to add other unsolicited information. A suggested service cycle for active listening follows:

- Maintain an open and inviting body posture.
- Look the person in the eye and send supportive signals (head nods, affirmatives).
- Briefly paraphrase their comments.

- Ask questions.
- Provide time for them to add more information by pausing before speaking.

The usefulness of this last item applies to adults as well as children. People will seek Doug out for private conversations about whatever is troubling them. He engages in all of these problem-solving and active listening techniques, especially using pauses. It no longer surprises him that people will often wait until the conversation is nearing its conclusion before they reveal a profound observation. Doug sometimes calls these "doorknob confessions" because they are often closest to the truth and the last thing people will tell you about when they seek you out. Hand on the doorknob to leave, they turn to tell you one more thing. "By the way, I almost forgot to mention…" and then here it comes. Be sure to give space in any conversation so that doorknob confessions can happen.

Action Research Tools Related to *Choice Words*

As you might have guessed, analyzing interactions between students and teachers is a difficult, yet important, task. Part of this difficulty relates to obtaining the necessary data and part of it relates to the very personal nature of analyzing interactions, especially interactions for which people might be defensive. Having said that, failure to engage in action research related to *choice words* would mean that the status quo has been accepted and that there is a fixed mindset about the interactions that teachers have, and the language they use, with their students. Communication is a defining element of any culture, and the words you choose will define much of yours! In this chapter, we offer three tools that might be useful in collecting data so that strengths can be recognized and improvements can be made.

The first tool, numbered 10 in the appendix, is a rubric useful in analyzing productive group work tasks. As we have noted, it's critical that students spend time interacting with one another and using language to figure things out. As Johnston (2004) notes, "when you figure something out for yourself, there is a certain thrill in the figuring. After a few successful experiences, you might start to think that figuring things out is something that you can actually do. Maybe you are even a figuring-out kind of person, encouraging an agentive dimension to identity" (p. 8), which is exactly what we hope happens in the classroom. We have found this rubric to be useful in reaching agreements with teachers about quality instruction and then using the tool for self-assessment and reflection as well as in conversations with peers, coaches, and administrators. Ensuring that the students are engaged in meaningful and significant tasks and conversations will go a long way in changing the power dynamics in the classroom.

Another tool that we have found useful requires that a video or audio sample of actual teaching be collected. We've tried to do this using field notes and scripts of observations, but we just miss too much of the context to have it be of much use. What we really need is the ability to slow down the process and thoughtfully review the interactions between teachers and students. In this way, we can begin to recognize the efforts teachers make in developing students' identity and agency. As you will see in action research tool 11, we only look for positive examples at first. We allow the absence of evidence to speak for itself when we talk with another person about the language that was used. Over time, when trust has been established, we note nonexamples as well as exemplars, and the conversation becomes much richer. Regardless, we can all set goals based on the analysis of video or audio recordings that allow us to update the language we use with students.

The third action research tool (number 12) related to *choice words* is a classroom observation guide. To use this tool, we suggest that you identify three specific students. These can be students who struggle with school, English-language learners, students who are quiet and typically nonparticipatory, or students who are gifted and who may not be challenged. You want to pick these students purposefully as you will examine interactions from the perspective of a specific set of students. The selection is not as important as the fact that the selected students should be from a group that the school is attending to for academic or social reasons. You'll want to observe the classroom interactions with the three targeted students in mind. We do not typically inform the classroom teacher which students we're observing so that the data collection is based on the natural interactions that adults have with students. There are a number of more formal tools you could use for this type of observation (e.g., TESA; http://www.lacoe.edu/orgs/165/index.cfm), but we recommend starting with some specific classroom interactions from the TESA framework, including these:

- Equitable response opportunities. Did the targeted students have an equal opportunity to respond to questions or participate in conversations as other students in the class? Are some students called on more often to participate?
- Affirmation. Did the targeted students receive an affirmation for their participation? Were these affirmations designed to build their agency and facilitate identity?
- Praise. Did the targeted students receive praise for their efforts? Were they positive and did the praise attribute success to the student?
- Wait time. Did the teacher wait at least five seconds after asking a targeted student a question before moving on, providing the answer, or calling on another student? Did the teacher wait at least two seconds after the student answered to invite elaboration?
- Proximity. Did the teacher get within arm's length of the targeted students during the lesson? Proximity communicates value and interest, and teachers should make an effort to come into close proximity with all of their students.

Conclusion

We are trying to create a culture that understands the damaging effect sarcasm can have on students who have yet to discover and celebrate who they are. We believe that in an attempt to be funny or make a point, the school staff may use sarcasm no differently than Maria's uncle did, and we believe the damage is just as great. We suggest that schools establish norms that limit the use of yelling, threatening, and sarcasm in adult-student interactions. It does nothing to establish trust, and it is very likely to cause significant pain. It will not establish a culture in which personal development is valued as a partner of educational success and helping students to find and be in their element. Inattentiveness can be equally damaging, as our rush to be heard ourselves can drown out the meaning students are attempting to convey through their words or actions. We cannot expect students to think about the future, create personal goals and achievement, find their passion, and appreciate their talents if their day is not formally structured beyond routinely demonstrating subject-matter competence. Pairing words and listening can make the power of "if" a reality. Developing identity, agency, and mindsets of achievement in students will help create a culture of achievement in your school. Choose your words wisely—they matter!

CHAPTER 5

It's Never Too Late to Learn

It's early summer, but high school guidance counselor Victor Suarez is already creating student schedules and class assignments for the incoming 9th graders from the district's middle schools. Mathematics is the quickest for him to do, so he begins there. "I can figure out pretty quickly how many sections we need for the pre-algebra, algebra, and geometry courses just by looking at student transcripts," he says. "Our district requires algebra in 8th grade," Mr. Suarez remarks, "so all I really need to do is figure out who passed it and who failed it. I put the kids who failed in 8th grade into the pre-algebra sections. The ones who passed it with a *B*, *C*, or *D* get algebra. All the ones with *A*s go into geometry."

Although Mr. Suarez is comfortable with his schedule-building system, his complacency is troubling. Robert Moses, founder of the Algebra Project, calls the access to algebra "a civil right" (2001, p. 6). For too many students, high school algebra is a gatekeeper course—if students don't get into algebra in 8th grade, they are on a path to low achievement in mathematics. To be sure, the effectiveness of requiring an algebra course in 8th grade is a mixed bag (Williams, Haertel, & Kirst, 2011). But a high school mathematics experience that begins with pre-algebra is more likely to result in a trajectory that will fail to lead to the kind of coursework required for admissions to most colleges and universities, if only because students run out of time. And if we as educators believe that all students should be "college-and career-ready," then we must have a plan for making them so, even when they arrive at our schoolhouse doors with skills deficits.

Presume Competence

Remember when you moved out of your childhood home and into your first adult living space? It's likely that your mother wondered whether you'd be able to sort your laundry and feed yourself, and your father doubted whether you'd be able to manage your finances. When Doug first moved out, he was nearly evicted because he failed to take care of the lawn of his rental home, a stipulation of his lease. Chances are very good that you made laundry, nutritional, financial, or caretaking errors in your first years of independent living. And yet the wiser people around you understood that making mistakes was a necessary, albeit painful, condition of learning. Most important, they presumed your competence from the beginning and did not confuse it with expertise. The presumption of competence requires a belief that a person possesses the basic ability to do something, however imperfectly.

On the first day of class, Benjamin Zander, maestro of the Boston Philharmonic, announces to each of his students that they are *A* students. As a condition of keeping their *A* for the semester, he has them write him a letter after the first class session, dated the last day of class, explaining why they earned their *A*. The letter discusses their attendance, hard work, and competent performance. Zander and Zander (2002) exemplify the concepts we will discuss in this chapter. They see possibility, and they presume competence. As we noted in the chapter on *choice words*, students project a story of their performance. It is fiction because it has yet to happen, but it can. It has possibility. Zander labels his students "outstanding students" before the class even begins and says, "This is the way I see you, and now tell me what you expect of yourself." It creates a mindset of achievement and a commitment to hard work to be an outstanding student. Students work hard, understanding it's never too late to learn, because their teacher assumes they can.

It's Never Too Late to Learn Pillar

The essential questions for this pillar challenge us to examine our beliefs about education: Are we willing to do what it takes to teach *all* the children in our schools? Do we place more value on compliance than competence? Can we develop systems that hold learning, not time, as the constant? Can we push students to go beyond the minimum needed to get by, to discover what they are capable of achieving?

The core philosophy behind the pillar "It's never too late to learn" is a presumption of competence. That does not mean that we believe that all students arrive on the first day of school with all the necessary skills and strategies they will need, but rather that they will develop competency under our tutelage. Presuming competence changes the way that teachers and students interact with each another. It also changes the opportunities that teachers provide for students (Jorgensen, McSheehan, & Sonnenmeier, 2007). We are reminded of Shantae, an African-American 3rd grader who lives in poverty, who once told a visitor to the class, "Do you wanna go to dinner tonight? We could trade in the pop bottles and go to Applebee's." There is tremendous evidence of resourcefulness in her response, as well interest in relationships with adults. However, if her teacher makes assumptions about her abilities based on her previous test scores or school records, she might never realize that Shantae is a ferocious reader who can weave amazing stories of characters and plots. Making an assumption that Shantae is not competent will limit what she is given to read and what she is invited to write about. It will also limit her future success because of the opportunities that are provided to her by the educational system.

Anchoring this tenet is a strong core of sound instructional practice. A school that concentrates its energy on repairing the fallout caused by poor teaching is fighting a losing battle, and one that will consume all of the school's human and fiscal resources in the process. For this reason, a school that places learning at its heart must view teaching, not remediation, as its primary focus. A business that defined its primary task as fixing its own faulty products rather than improving the quality of its production is doomed in the marketplace. After all, who would purchase a lousy product with great customer service? And who would invest in such an organization? The business of school is teaching and learning, and it requires fierce and unwavering focus.

A Framework for Instructional Excellence

Learning doesn't just happen, and neither does good teaching. And although educators will roundly criticize a transmission model of teaching, in practice it occurs more often than most of us would care to admit (Gill & Hoffman, 2009). With time as a limited resource, teachers resort to covering topics, rather than uncovering them (Wiggins & McTighe, 2005). The pressure to make sure all the standards of a content area are addressed can cause many to concede the territory of best practices. "At least I got them ready for the state test," they say in an effort to reconcile these conflicting demands.

But the field of learning sciences makes it clear that learning is different from training, and that our ultimate goal is to promote transfer within and across courses, disciplines, and settings. After all, learning is ultimately the ability to use a skill when not otherwise prompted to do so. When 7th grader Rebecca mentally calculates the savings she will receive on a marked-down item at the thrift store, she is using math. When 11th grader Jorge reads an online music review and questions whether the blogger was really objective, given that the website is sponsored by a record label, he is using literacy skills.

In their book *How People Learn*, authors Bransford, Brown, and Cocking (2000) note that "transfer is affected by the degree to which people learn with understanding rather than merely memorize sets of facts or follow a fixed set of procedures" (p. 55). In order for students to successfully transfer their learning to new situations, they need time to recognize patterns, opportunities to use metacognitive thinking, experiences with success, and opportunities to apply what they have learned in new situations (Bransford et al., 2000).

So what does this mean for instructional design? Teaching for transfer requires a clear process for establishing purpose, exposure to the thinking processes of experts, scaffolded instruction, and ample opportunity to clarify understanding through productive group work. With a solid grounding, students are able to use this knowledge independently. It also requires that transfer be fostered *within* the learning experiences. This process, known as a gradual release of responsibility (Pearson & Gallagher, 1983), was first articulated in reading instruction (shared, guided, and independent reading). We have expanded both the model and its context through a gradual release of responsibility instructional framework that is useful across disciplines (Fisher & Frey, 2008a). See figure 5.1 for an illustration of this process.

FIGURE 5.1

Gradual Release of Responsibility Instructional Framework

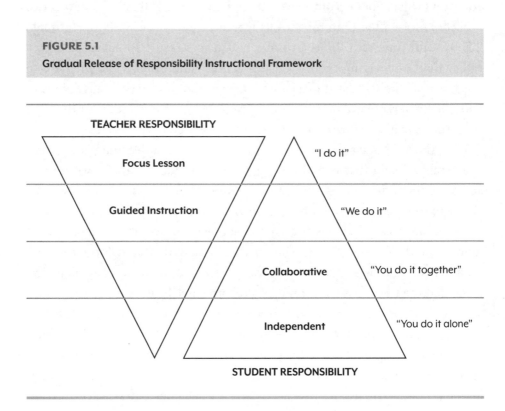

The focus lesson. The introduction of a concept or skill is a critical time for learning. It requires establishing relevance so that students can situate their learning within a context. We call this establishing purpose, and it really comes down to this simple statement: "Here's what we're going to learn about today, and here's what I want you to do with it" (Fisher & Frey, 2011).

The evidence is that a well-established purpose is useful for all students, and especially for English-language learners (Hill & Flynn, 2006). After establishing purpose, the teacher models or demonstrates the concept or skill, interjecting it with think-aloud statements to expose students to expert thinking.

For example, 2nd grade teacher Misty Mendenhall uses the concrete poem "The Salmon" with its accompanying illustration of three spawning salmon swimming up a fish ladder in a waterfall (Florian, 1997). After reading the poem, she says,

> One of the things I noticed right away is that I have to read this poem from the bottom to the top of the page. I saw that the words were slanted at the same angle as the picture of the fish on the opposite page [*traces the angle of the text and the picture with her finger*]. I also noticed that the poet used lots of exclamation marks. Look, there are seven! [*Points and counts*] Hmm, I've decided that the main emotion the poet wants me to feel is excitement and leaping upward like the salmon. I decided this because the illustration, the angle of the text, and the exclamation points all point upward.

By thinking aloud, Ms. Mendenhall was able to model her reading comprehension of the poem in order to make inferences about the poet's intended message. Her use of the word "because" is crucial in that it foregrounds her decision-making process. Without this justification, students do not gain much insight beyond the decision itself. The choice to make her decision-making process transparent is the first step in the transfer of learning.

Guided instruction. This phase of instruction is likely where the gradual release of responsibility got its name, because it is a perfect description of what occurs. Once initial instruction has happened in the focus lesson, the teacher needs to determine what students know and do not know. It is unrealistic to expect that all the students learned everything the first time it was presented. But what have they retained, and what have they missed? That's why guided instruction is important as a formative assessment, as it allows the teacher to determine what needs to be retaught, as well as when it is time to move on (Frey & Fisher, 2011).

Guided instruction is also the phase when scaffolded instruction can happen. This is accomplished through the strategic use of robust questions to check for understanding, and cognitive and metacognitive prompts to remind students to use what they know to resolve problems. When these prompts are not successful, visual and verbal cues are used to shift the learner's attention to the information source that he or she needs. If the student is still unable to arrive at a solution, the teacher temporarily reassumes cognitive responsibility by modeling, demonstrating, and thinking aloud, as in the focus lesson. Importantly, the teacher then shifts the tack back to the learner once again by saying, "Now you try it."

It's analogous to a dance. Whether it is a foxtrot or a salsa, there are basic steps that must be mastered. But the artistry comes in combining those dance steps in unique ways. That is why scripted programs often fail to deliver on claims. The omission of guided instruction makes it far more difficult for a teacher to artfully scaffold student learning and address misconceptions and partial understandings. A common misconception about guided instruction is that it can only be accomplished during extended small-group instruction. It's true that guided instruction is often confused with guided reading, leaving secondary and content-area teachers wondering how this could happen. We'll hold that question for a few moments while we discuss a related element of a structured teaching framework: collaborative learning.

Collaborative learning. This is the phase of instruction that really succeeds in promoting metacognitive thinking as students work in the company of peers to clarify and refine their understanding of concepts and skills. In particular, students are able to notice when they are having difficulty with a task. In too many cases, we've had students nod eagerly when we've asked, "Does that make sense?" only to discover later that it didn't. The tasks students are working on should promote productive group work that exposes what they do and do not know. The notion of productive failure is one that first emerged in mathematics instruction for middle school learners (Kapur, 2008). In essence, its advocates theorize that by deliberately causing errors in a learning situation, students focus their attention on the error and are more able to assimilate subsequent instruction about avoiding the error. Those wise people who supported our moves to our first adult living arrangements would put it another way: "You learn from your mistakes."

Therefore, the task design is crucial; too easy and the group subdivides it and goes their separate ways, reuniting only for assembly. Make it too hard and they give up altogether. An ideal collaborative learning task results in lots of discussion and interaction among group members as they use what they collectively know. They ask questions of one another, justify their answers, and apply their social skills to resolve problems. And here's where guided instruction comes in: the teacher moves from group to group, asking robust questions to check for understanding, providing prompts and cues to scaffold instruction, and temporarily retreating to the direct instruction of the focus lesson when needed to reteach.

A case in point: Sixth grade social studies teacher Carl Burgess has moved his students in small groups to complete a poster on an element of life in ancient Egypt. As he approaches one group, he hears them discussing differences between girls and boys of the time. He asks them, "I know you've been talking about gender differences, but I'm wondering if class made a difference, too?"

Jordan replies, "You mean like rich kids and poor kids?"

"Exactly," says the teacher. "Do you have any information about this already?" Nuri immediately begins looking in her textbook. "I remember we read about the pharaohs, scribes, farmers, and slaves," she mutters. "It's here somewhere...oh, here it is!" As Nuri reads the passage aloud, Jordan and Ofelia lean closer to listen. Mr. Burgess prompts them by saying, "I would make a chart of similarities and differences between the classes first..." when Ofelia exclaims, "and then we could find out about boys and girls in each group!" In a matter of a few minutes, the teacher has used guided instruction within a collaborative learning setting to scaffold their learning. With that, Mr. Burgess moves to the next group. Not to be overlooked is the transfer that just took place as the students applied their collective knowledge of texts and graphic organizers to create a framework for their inquiry.

Independent learning. As students approach mastery, they are able to assume even more cognitive responsibility. In the past, this might have consisted of worksheets (we like to call them "shut-up sheets") that were primarily used to maintain a quiet and orderly classroom. The field has moved beyond this, and administrators and teachers are in wide agreement that a quiet classroom isn't necessarily a learning one.

The independent phase of learning can be divided into two segments: within the class and outside the class, better known as homework. We'll reserve a discussion of homework for later in this chapter and instead focus here on the formative assessment opportunities that are present for both. Too often, independent work is seen as a summative assessment event. The student works alone, the teacher grades it, the student gets it back, and then we all move on to a new topic. There is a place for summative assessment, but it isn't while learning is still happening. Rather, students who are working independently should still have opportunities to get feedback and revise their work. The logistics of this will vary according to content and developmental levels but include these:

- Peer responses to writing
- Conferences with the teacher to discuss independent reading
- Holding a conversation with the teacher in a world language class
- Completing a checklist to report on one's progress for a longer project
- Recording a presentation and uploading it to the classroom wiki for comment by peers and the teacher

Each of these examples provides a space for feedback, discussion, and revision. In addition, it provides learners with the opportunity to transfer their learning to novel situations. Although students are moving closer to mastery, they are not quite ready for the summative evaluations of grading. We'll discuss that topic next.

Grading for Competence or Compliance?

Reducing everything known about a student's performance to a letter is a daunting task, yet teachers do it every day. Some have sophisticated and complicated systems with percentages and weighting factors to determine students' grades, while others have systems in which students rack up points, much like a pinball game. Regardless of the specific system used, grades are a touchy subject and one that causes a great deal of debate. After all, grades are the gatekeepers for whether a student will attend a prestigious college or repeat a course. What we do know is that grading is often fairly subjective, with varying mixtures of effort, participation, homework completion, and citizenship added to the brew (O'Connor, 2009). The same student in one class might earn a satisfactory grade yet in another class with a different teacher might earn an exemplary grade for the same work.

There have been a number of attempts to address this issue, including getting groups of teachers together to examine student work. This process of collaborative analysis has resulted in better alignment of expectations and evaluation of student work (Langer, Colton, & Goff, 2003). Other efforts have focused on eliminating the *D* grade (Reynolds, 2010), not giving zeros due to the fact that they have a disproportionate impact on student grades (Reeves, 2011), and creating standards-based report cards (Guskey, 2008). While each of these efforts has had some positive effects, the question about grading remains: what do we grade?

Determining what we want students to know and be able to do is an important part of the teaching and learning process. Advice from experts suggests that our planning process should "begin with the end in mind" (Covey, 2004). In education, we begin with the end in mind using a process called *Understanding by Design* (Wiggins & McTighe, 2005). This process has three major components:

1. Identify desired results.
2. Determine acceptable evidence.
3. Plan learning experiences and instruction.

This process has been described elsewhere and has been implemented in school systems all over the world. Our pillar *it's never too late to learn* forced us to examine, in greater detail, the second major component in *Understanding by Design*. We had to ask ourselves, what is acceptable evidence of student learning?

If a 2nd grader completed all of the take-home worksheets, should her teacher accept that as evidence for learning? If a middle school student can perform well on state standards tests, is that acceptable evidence for learning? And if a teacher can describe a new instructional routine after attending a professional development event, is that evidence of learning? Do we have any proof that the information will be used? In each of these cases, we would argue that the burden of proof was not met.

Although each of these conventional systems for collecting evidence provide teachers with information, they are not all useful in determining student mastery. Too often, we have confused compliance with competence. For example, in Doug's math class in high school, 25 percent of the grade was based on homework completion, 25 percent was based on a notebook that required that he copy notes as the teacher lectured, and 50 percent was based on unit tests. Think about the implications from this system in terms of grades and the identification of needed instruction. Let's say that Doug passed every test with an A but refused to do the homework or take notes. In this case, Doug was competent but not compliant, and he would fail the class. Alternatively, if Doug was compliant and not competent, he could pass the class by copying the homework from a peer, taking notes in class or copying from peers, and then getting poor grades on the tests.

In other cases, families are graded. Access to support at home in the form of a knowledgeable adult who can provide the time, physical space, and tutelage needed when the homework is difficult cannot be assumed. To see it as only a question of economics doesn't go far enough. This type of home support can be found in wealthy communities as well as poor ones. Certainly wage earners working multiple jobs, crowded housing, and childcare issues should not be overlooked. But family circumstances play a role across household income levels. Single-parent homes, tired adults, health crises, and older siblings with their own burdens can be found in every neighborhood. Any of these circumstances can increase the likelihood that the homework will not be completed on a given night. Should a family's difficulties have a magnified effect on the child's grade? To ensure that teachers know which students need additional instruction and support, we have to separate competence from compliance. This realization led us to the development of competencies as a way to begin with the end in mind, determining the acceptable evidence for student learning while reducing the unintended effects of family circumstances that can make homework completion tasks unpredictable.

Building a Competence-Based System

While there are many who question the value of grades, especially when they are used to bribe students to complete work (e.g., Kohn, 1999), when grades are given they should reflect students' understanding of the content. Grades are abbreviated information about a student's performance in a specific subject and should reflect a level of mastery of the content taught.

If grades are to reflect mastery of the content, then teachers have to begin by analyzing the content standards and discussing their essential components. From there, teachers can design assessment tools that ascertain what students know. Given that there is a wide range of methods to determine student understanding (Popham, 2010), teachers can develop a diverse set of measures. Some competencies can be traditional tests with a mixture of multiple-choice and short-answer items, which is one way that students are expected to demonstrate their understanding. Parenthetically, this is important because students are expected to demonstrate their understanding using this genre on state accountability measures as well. But tests are not the only way to assess student learning. In addition, there can be competencies that involve oral presentations, projects, performances, and writing. Here is a sample of competencies:

- A 20-page graphic novel retelling the events of the French Revolution, either inked by the student or using imported images
- A 1,500-word essay and a creative component (such as an iMovie or original song) in response to the essential question "Can you buy your way to happiness?"
- A 25-item exam on polynomials with written explanations of the problem-solving procedures used for 10 of the questions
- The development of a crime cell story in which the crime is solved using knowledge of DNA, RNA, and genetics

A competency for kindergartners in reading might be to identify lower- and uppercase letters and their corresponding sounds. This outcome will require quality instruction and learning experiences, including teacher modeling, direct and explicit instruction, group work, independent tasks, and guided instruction. Simply participating in the learning activities, however, should not be confused with mastery or the need for supplemental intervention. Instead, planning with an expectation that all students will demonstrate this level of understanding leads the teacher to specific learning activities that are based on what students already know and can do.

Competencies represent the expected outcomes, and teachers can plan backward to design the scope and sequence of daily lessons. This provides teachers with an authentic opportunity to implement the concepts from *Understanding by Design* (Wiggins & McTighe, 2005) as they already have identified the enduring understandings that were important to them. As teachers plan lessons to ensure that students pass the competencies, they will naturally develop activities, tasks, and assignments that allow students to practice, and receive feedback about their efforts, in advance of demonstrating their competency. This will likely raise the question about practice work. Should practice work contribute to students' grades, or should grades be based entirely on students' demonstration of understanding as measured on the competencies?

When schools move to a competency-based system, they often have to examine a number of their traditions and policies. For example, if grades are to be based on demonstrated competency, what role does homework play? Furthermore, if students do not pass the competency, what actions should the teacher or school take?

Academic Recovery: All Hands on Deck

When a student does not pass a competency, it should be taken as a sign that the student needs additional instruction to master the content. As such, we recommend that the student receive the score of "incomplete" (*I*) rather than *F*. Telling a student "you failed" can interfere with the student-teacher relationship, which is one of the things that the "failure is not an option" effort tried to address. Instead, when students are told that their effort or performance is incomplete, they understand that they will receive additional support so they can learn the content and demonstrate their understanding of the subject matter.

In general, we recommend that academic recovery focus on students who score below 70 percent on any competency. While there are a number of different options teachers and students have relative to the actions to take when students score below 70 percent, most of these actions involve supplemental intervention. As such, competencies can serve as a progress-monitoring tool that triggers tier 2 (or tier 3) supplemental and intensive interventions in an RTI model. For example, when Miriam scored 54 percent on her Westward Expansion competency, her teacher knew that she needed additional instruction. This came in the form of additional small-group instruction and participation in an after-school tutorial program. When she did not make progress after several weeks of this intervention and started amassing additional incompletes on tasks involving content reading, the teacher referred Miriam to the school RTI team. Miriam needed intensive interventions in the area of reading informational text to be successful in the competency systems used in her elementary school.

In secondary schools, students are typically allowed two weeks after the date of the competency to take care of matters on their own. At the end of the two-week period, students who still have an incomplete in the grade book are assigned lunchtime and after-school tutorials (Fisher, Frey, & Grant, 2009).

Providing academic recovery services requires a commitment on the part of the entire school staff. This can't be overlooked in the rush to put such a program in place. In our experience, teachers can view such efforts quite positively in theory, only to have those beliefs challenged when it comes to students and the academic work required in their classes. "When we first started talking about [academic recovery], I thought it was a great idea," one mathematics teacher told us. "After all, who would be opposed to more student support? But then I got pretty defensive when I had all these students fail a competency and it was public knowledge. It was like 'You're not a good teacher.' No one said that, of course, but that's the way I felt. It took me a while to realize that my ego was getting in the way of learning."

A way to overcome this is for the teacher and student to craft an academic recovery plan like the one in figure 5.2. By locating the conversation first at this level, both are left feeling empowered by the discussion. Parent involvement is also crucial to understand how they can support their child's efforts, such as scheduling before- or after-school tutorials and providing a quiet time and place to work at home, if possible. These contracts are coordinated by an appointed academic recovery person to oversee these efforts and to produce a weekly list of students for the staff. These publicized lists make it possible for other adults at the school to extend the encouragement and support that students need beyond the content teacher. As more than one student has commented, "Everyone knows my business. But I guess that's in a good way."

Academic recovery isn't only for students who have not yet demonstrated their mastery of the content—it is also for students who have passed but want to do better. In the four years that we have offered academic recovery at our high school, 28 percent of the participating students are there to improve a passing grade. While 70 percent is the cutoff for earning a passing grade, we want to push students to move beyond minimal compliance to strive for a higher level of mastery. In some cases, this requires lots of encouragement. "Sometimes I have a conversation with a student about their passing score, and invite them to consider whether they would like to find out what they're capable of doing," says advanced mathematics teacher Dina Burow. "A score of 82 percent on a competency may be adequate, but in some cases they skated by on what they knew, without really digging down to find out how their effort could pay off."

Ms. Burow's point is well worth considering. In preparing students for postsecondary and workplace experiences, just getting by isn't enough. Competition is fierce for college enrollment spots and for jobs, and some students may have little personal resolve for digging deeper by investing more time and effort. Making it possible for students to retake alternative versions of competencies for grade improvement encourages a sense of risk taking. "There are those students who fear failure even more than they desire excellence," said Ms. Burow. "When they know they can't hurt their grade, only help it, they're more willing to take risks as a learner."

Whether students participate in academic recovery to clear an incomplete or to improve a passing grade, the school's achievement level is raised. Think about how standardized tests are situated within the learning lives of students. Conventional wisdom holds that students learn and then

FIGURE 5.2

Academic Recovery Plan

STUDENT NAME: _____

DATE OF CONFERENCE: _____

COURSE NAME: _____

Grade I received: _____　　Grade I would like to earn through completion of this plan: _____

What did I have the most difficulty with in this class?

What do I need to do to raise my grade?	Who can help me?	Date

What is my first step in achieving my goal of academic recovery?

_____　_____　_____
　　　Student Signature　　　　　　　　Parent Signature　　　　　　　Teacher Signature

Source: Fisher, D., & Frey, N. (2010). *Enhancing RTI: How to ensure success with effective classroom instruction and intervention.* Alexandria, VA: ASCD. Used with permission.

demonstrate their learning on a big test, and the collective results say something about the school's efforts. But what about students who don't learn the first time around or who only partially learn the content? Without a system in place to increase their learning beyond classroom instruction, learning is fixed and static, and there is little chance that it will change. Alternatively, an academic recovery system ensures that those who didn't learn the first time around must persist, and those who did well enough can move from adequate to excellent. These sustained efforts hold learning as the constant and time as the variable. The investment pays off in the form of standardized measures of a school because those who wouldn't have learned received further opportunities to do so. And those who learned enough to get by have the chance to move from good to great. If we're going to accept that standardized test scores are in part a measure of a school's effort, then let's shift our efforts to improving learning beyond the classroom.

The school's commitment to academic recovery extends to the focus of the entire staff. As discussed in the *welcome* chapter, those not traditionally involved in daily instruction play an important role in the life of the school. Academic recovery efforts require the support and encouragement of *all* the adults. An administrator who rolls up her sleeves to work with students in a lunchtime tutorial session conveys the message that nothing is more important than learning. The front desk person who asks a student worker about his academic recovery plan for the week demonstrates interest in his progress. A technology coordinator who redirects visiting students to their after-school tutorial shows that he knows about the learning efforts of the school.

At Wren Falls Elementary, grade-level teachers have developed a schedule for providing academic recovery supports for all students, regardless of the child's teacher. "When we first starting offering academic recovery, the child worked directly with his or her teacher. But we quickly found out that *that* didn't work!" said 4th grade teacher Ivy Williams. "The child might come to our before-school tutorial, only to discover that her teacher wasn't there that particular morning. And there might not even be another teacher there from the child's grade level." Ms. Williams went on to describe an improved system. "We now make sure that the tutorial room has all the materials needed for all the competencies for each grade level," she said. "Now if a kindergarten pupil shows up, I can help him with the math competency he's working on. I just go to the file drawer and pull out all the materials I need, including practice work and the competency itself. It's made it a lot more seamless for students."

Students play an active role in academic recovery efforts, especially in setting goals for themselves. This is another essential aspect of the *it's never too late to learn* pillar. Students need to take ownership of their improvement efforts. Ninth grade English teacher Kelly Johnson designed a goal-setting form for each student in academic recovery to complete prior to beginning the session. "I want them to be invested in this process," she said. "It can't be enough that they're doing this strictly for someone else, because that doesn't foster the intrinsic motivation they need to achieve. Plus, it helps me figure out how to organize supports when there's a roomful of students here."

Homework as a Tool for Learning

A conversation about grading and academic recovery inevitably leads to one about homework, a topic that prompts lots of strong feelings. The debate is filled with strong voices in favor of, as well as opposed to, homework. Each voice cites typical concerns about the need for homework (provides a practice effect, builds character) as well as the need to abolish it (detracts from family time, doesn't result in better grades.) Hattie's (2009) meta-analysis of 800 educational practices (including homework) reveals a mixed bag on the subject of homework. The overall effects are moderately positive but include some important caveats:

- More effective at the high school level, with almost no effect at the elementary level
- More effective in math, but less effective in social studies and science
- Time matters: shorter is better than longer
- Does not result in time management skills
- Better when it is not complex and does not require higher-level thinking skills.

For us, there are two major concerns about homework. One is that a gradual release of responsibility instructional framework must be applied to homework as well. If one acknowledges that the independent phase of instruction should come only after students are well on their way to mastery, then out-of-school independent homework should be similarly aligned. Unlike the 28 percent of teachers who reported that they often or very often assigned homework based on what they didn't get to complete in class (Markow, Kim, & Liebman, 2007), teachers should assign homework that reviews the familiar, providing learners with time for

- *Fluency building* (e.g., independent reading, timed math computation drills);
- *Application of learned skills* (e.g., measuring household items to find out what is one foot in length);
- *Spiral review* (e.g., reviewing previously taught information that will be useful for an upcoming unit);
- *Extension* (e.g., establishing a Facebook page on a worthy cause one has been researching in school; Fisher & Frey, 2008b).

In addition to the design of the homework, a second concern is the way the assignments are used. A grading system that allows for homework completion to influence grading to varying degrees builds resentment among students, families, and teachers. In addition to raising questions of fairness (Reeves, 2011), it obscures what students really know and undermines grades as a useful, rather than punitive, feedback system. In addition, it drains the limited fiscal and human resources of a school that must devote precious time to addressing the failing grades of its students. In short, it would seem far more logical to dedicate our joint efforts to matters of learning, rather than compliance.

The complexities of coming to agreement about matters of grading, academic recovery, and homework cannot be underestimated. When aligned, policies and procedures become easier to design and implement. But when there isn't a will to bring these challenging topics out in the open, practices develop in a haphazard fashion and school becomes an obstacle course instead of a place to learn.

Organizational Principles

In creating a culture in which it's never too late to learn, there are a number of organizational principles that can be operationalized through service cycles. To start, we have provided principles we have found effective. Of course, each school will need to customize this list and develop principles that guide its work.

1. *All students deserve high-quality instruction.*
2. *Learning is not fixed in time. Learning should be the constant, with time being a variable.*
3. *Learning is often like writing a letter—it may take several drafts to get it right. Perseverance is an attribute of success that will be supported and rewarded at our school.*
4. *Recognize competence, not compliance.*
5. *Rigor means students are challenged, but not frustrated to the point of giving up.*
6. *Rally resources when students exhibit gaps in performance. In other words, "all hands on deck" when student competency is not demonstrated.*
7. *Every adult in the school has an instructional role, including recovery and support efforts.*
8. *Grades don't teach—people do!*

These organizational principles guide the interactions we have with colleagues, visitors, and students. In addition, we see these as critical to the long-term achievement of students because they provide flexible, just-in-time support while also ensuring rigor in the curriculum. When students understand that it's never too late to learn, they are willing to take risks to push themselves and know that they can recover from the mistakes that they make during the learning process.

Putting Principles into Action with Service Cycles

As we noted in chapter 2, service cycles help institutionalize behaviors such that they become the norm of the school. Several service cycles are useful in the implementation of the belief that *it's never too late to learn*. Of course, this is also a much more philosophical belief for teachers, more so than *welcome* or *do no harm*. Accordingly, it is important to have reflective conversations with teachers about student learning. Do people believe that there are a finite number of *As* that can be given? Do people believe that time is fixed and, thus, if competency isn't demonstrated in October, it's too late to do so? These beliefs get in the way of this pillar and have to be addressed first. If you work at a school in which personal beliefs are getting in the way, we draw your attention to the professional development and professional learning communities work that needs to be done. This is the focus of chapter 7. You might need to start there, if people do not inherently believe that every student can achieve at high levels or that time is a fixed commodity. Assuming that the faculty is open to a conversation about the implementation of this pillar, we suggest paying attention to the following service cycles. Of course, there will be additional service cycles that you'll want to implement based on the history and culture of your school.

Consistent implementation of high-quality instruction. As we have discussed previously, access to high-quality instruction is required if students are to reach high levels of achievement. Furthermore, it is worth repeating: schools cannot focus all of their efforts on remediation or on academic recovery, for that matter. Doing so would tax the fiscal and human resources available to a school. As evidenced in the response to instruction and intervention work (Fisher & Frey, 2010), schools must pay attention to quality core instruction, thereby reducing the number of students who require supplemental and intensive interventions.

At the minimum, there are five components required of every lesson:

- A clearly stated *purpose* that focuses on what students are expected to learn
- Teacher *modeling*, in which students are exposed to the thinking of experts
- *Collaborative learning* tasks that provide students with opportunities to work productively with their peers and for which they are individually accountable
- Strategic use of questions, prompts, and cues that *guide* students to deeper understanding

- *Independent learning* tasks, both in class and at home, that are linked with previous learning and provide students with an opportunity to apply what they have learned

In some schools, there are additions to these five components that teachers and administrators agree will be part of the quality core instruction. Examples include these:

- Writing across the curriculum—students are expected to complete a number of writing tasks in every subject area, and teachers use student writing to check for understanding.
- Systematic vocabulary development in which students are taught specialized and technical words in advance of a lesson and then are expected to use these targeted words in their collaborative and independent tasks.
- Inquiry or problem-based learning that provides students opportunities to ask questions and wonder about the curriculum.

When teachers in a school routinely and regularly implement this service cycle, students develop habits and their achievement improves (Frey, Fisher, & Nelson, 2010). When there is evidence that this service cycle is not being implemented, professional development and coaching are warranted. For example, when Principal Gloria Diaz walked through all of the classrooms in her school, she was pleased to hear teachers modeling their thinking and students working collaboratively. In one classroom, for example, she observed a group of 4th graders solving math problems. They were working in groups of three. One person in the group was solving the problem with numbers, another person with words, and the third person visually or graphically. When each member of the group had completed his or her task, they shared their ideas and asked each other questions. Ms. Diaz was pleased to see that students used sentence frames designed to facilitate their argumentation skills, such as when Ernesto said, "I agree with you because 1/5 of the apple means that it is smaller than the whole apple" or when Giselle asked, "How did you get that answer? Show me because mine is different."

Ms. Diaz asked the group of students, "What are you learning?" but was not satisfied with their responses, which focused on what they were doing, not what they were learning. And some of the students did not even know that. As Deon said, "I don't know. We just gotta do these problems." This led Ms. Diaz to question the purpose-setting component of this service cycle. She scheduled a schoolwide conversation on the value of purpose and shared her classroom walkthrough findings. She shared some video clips that she collected during the day in which students responded to the question "What are you learning today and why?" She was not mad at the faculty, and she did not tell them that they were "bad" teachers. Rather, she asked them why having a purpose that focused on learning was important and how they might work together to improve that aspect of their service cycle. One of the action research tools, presented later in this chapter, is the classroom observation tool that Ms. Diaz uses.

Competencies and other formative assessments. Beginning with the end in mind is a wise practice and one that has become institutionalized in the planning process of teachers who use *Understanding by Design* (Wiggins & McTighe, 2005). In essence, teachers who understand this process know that they have to determine what they want students to know and be able to do as a result of the instruction. They also know that their instruction should be driven by student understanding and that formative assessment tools are useful in helping teachers plan. We use the term "competencies" to describe what students should know and be able to do, and we note that they can be used both formatively and summatively. When teachers use competencies formatively, they provide students with instruction and intervention based on performance. For example, when a student does not demonstrate competency in multiplying fractions, additional instruction, and perhaps intervention, will be implemented. Competencies can also be used summatively to generate report card and grading information. Having said that, it's important to note that *it's never too late to learn* suggests that students can retake competencies to demonstrate increased mastery and that their grades should change accordingly.

We have already provided an example of a competency, so we will focus this service cycle on the components of a competency, or other formative assessment. The following list is not exhaustive, but rather should be used to develop a system for using assessment information to determine which students require additional instruction or intervention.

- There are multiple ways for demonstrating knowledge, and the competencies should tap into those various ways. For a given subject area, one competency could be multiple choice and the next could be a project or an essay.
- Competencies should align with the standards being taught.
- Some of the competencies should resemble the tasks students are asked to do relative to accountability measures. After all, tests are a genre that will exist in learners' lives for years to come. If you doubt that, think about getting a driver's license or admission into college.
- There should be grade-level or course-alike agreement about the content and format for each competency.
- The content of the competency should guide teachers in determining which students need what content retaught.
- Competencies should be designed in advance of instruction so that teachers begin with the end in mind.
- Recognize excellence for those who do well on competencies.

Recognition of excellence is a part of our service cycle for competencies. We want to convey our pride in their achievement and give families a cause for celebration. Doug and Nancy write letters of congratulations for students who have scored well on a competency. When classroom teachers give us the names of these students, we handwrite and hand-address a card to the student that has been printed for this purpose. We've heard stories of how these cards are used at home, with some families displaying them on the refrigerator or on a wall space dedicated to these cards. Other students have told us that their family uses the letters as an occasion to go out for a celebratory meal together or even as a chance to give kids a monetary reward (not something that we encourage, but families are entitled to their own ways of recognizing their child's work). It's an interesting dynamic for families of adolescents, who are often reticent to discuss school matters with their families, and we're happy to give students a reason to have such a positive conversation.

Academic recovery efforts. When student learning falls short of expectations, the academic recovery efforts must kick in. If students have demonstrated that they have not yet mastered content, we cannot simply average their scores and say they are passing or, worse, fail them and require that they try again next year. Instead, the school system must have a service cycle in place to respond when students fail. And this response must be planned in advance so that each individual in the school knows what his or her role is when it comes to academic recovery.

This service cycle requires that there is a system for completing each of the following tasks, routinely:

- Weekly identification of students who have not yet demonstrated competency
- Scheduling recovery efforts, such as during class time, during lunch, or before and after school
- Scheduling staffing for each of the recovery times
- Determining which funds are available to support the academic recovery efforts
- Identifying roles and responsibilities for each staff member relative to academic recovery, whether that be reminding students to attend, supervising tutoring efforts, mentoring students in a motivational way, or compiling the lists of who needs recovery
- Recognizing excellence and effort of students involved in the academic recovery program

At Wren Falls Elementary, the reading specialist attends all grade-level meetings. As part of the meeting, teachers identify students who have yet to reach competency. The reading specialist compiles the list from these meetings and then sends the list out weekly to all teachers, not just those on the grade-level team. This log is updated; when students demonstrate competency, their name is removed from the list and a recognition letter is sent home.

Students on the list are contacted personally, typically by a paraprofessional who has been trained in advocacy techniques. The role of this paraprofessional is to elicit a commitment from the student to attend recovery efforts of his or her choice. The paraprofessional also communicates with family members, letting them know that their child will be receiving additional instruction and in which subject areas.

At Wren Falls, academic recovery occurs during class time and is provided by a group of adults, including the classroom teacher, reading specialist, counselor, and speech therapist. As students in the class work collaboratively, students who have yet to master the competencies receive additional instruction from one of these adults. In addition, there is an after-school program funded by the U.S. Department of Education that provides students with additional tutoring and mentoring. The reading specialist meets with the after-school program director each week to discuss students' needs and interventions.

As with competencies, students in academic recovery also benefit from recognition. Ian writes letters to every student who clears an incomplete or uses this opportunity for grade improvement. He calls these "grit letters" to recognize the perseverance, determination, and resolve of students who embody the belief that it truly is never too late to learn. This practice is influenced by the work of Duckworth, Peterson, Matthews, and Kelly (2007), who have examined the relationship between these "grit" attributes and achievement and who have found, quite simply, that "gritty students outperform their less gritty peers" (p. 1093). We witnessed the payoff to fostering grit when Anndy, in the late spring of his senior year, jubilantly ran down the hallway with his last math competency of his high school career. Anndy had been a student at our school for four years, and in all of that time he had to retake every math competency he ever had. He never passed one of them on his first try. But this day was different. "I passed it the FIRST time!" he exclaimed. Anndy got a grit letter from Ian that night, as well as a card congratulating him on his achievement from Doug.

It really is never too late to learn.

Action Research Tools Related to It's Never Too Late to Learn

Once again, take a good look around your school. Is competence based on what you can learn in a certain amount of time, or is demonstrating competence a partnership between students and teachers that involves quality instruction and sustained effort? Does the wherewithal and resolve exist in your school to teach students to persevere until they demonstrate the competencies they need to achieve? We suggest tools here that can help you take an objective look at whether learning at your school is always a work in progress or whether it is over for some students. As you use these tools and look at whether it is too late for students, think about the gap between that reality and your mission, beliefs, and purpose. What organizational principles do you need to focus on, and what service cycles may reengage students in their learning, performance, and achievement? After you look at what is happening and think about what you might do to be more effective educators, put those principles and cycles into practice. *It's never too late to learn* is a pillar that is fundamental to a culture of achievement because you will purposefully act in ways that encourage engagement and eliminate reasons for apathy and withdrawal.

As we have noted, this pillar is based on teachers' core beliefs. A good starting point, to determine teachers' beliefs, is the administration of a learning attitude survey. We have included a sample survey in the appendix, action research tool 13. We have used this survey with teachers from elementary to high school with good results. We recommend administering this anonymously and tabulating results at the aggregate level to determine if there are areas of need. Of course, you should feel comfortable changing the questions on the attitude survey to match the history of your school and the efforts that have been undertaken. Regardless of the specific questions you ask, it is important to determine the core beliefs that teachers have relative to instruction and intervention. If the attitudes are not conducive to the culture that needs to be created, we suggest starting with professional readings in a learning community. More information about this can be found in chapter 7, but here are a few readings that we have found powerful to engage school staffs in this conversation:

- *The Art of Possibility: Transforming Professional and Personal Life* (Zander & Zander, 2002, Penguin Books)
- *Rethinking Homework: Best Practices That Support Diverse Needs* (Vatterott, 2009, ASCD)

- *Better Learning Through Structure Teaching: A Framework for the Gradual Release of Responsibility* (Fisher & Frey, 2008, ASCD)

A second action research tool that we have found useful in the implementation of this pillar is the classroom walkthrough tool developed by Dr. Page Dettmann in Sarasota Schools, Florida (action research tool 14). This tool, aligned with the phases of gradual release of responsibility, can provide you with information about areas of high implementation and areas of instructional need. In addition to providing individual teachers with feedback, the results from many observations can be analyzed for patterns that guide school improvement efforts.

A third action research tool (number 15) involves homework and the practices that teachers are currently using. This tool provides information about average completion rates of homework, as well as the type of homework being given. Analyzing this data can lead to fruitful conversations about the role that homework should play in students' learning. This tool requires data be analyzed concerning the number and percentages of students who complete the assigned homework task versus those who do not, or who do not do so correctly. In addition, this tool requires an analysis of the type of task students were asked to complete. There are other types of homework tasks than those listed on the form, but those other types of tasks have less evidence for their usefulness. Analyzing the task in this way can result in conversations about needed changes in homework and the strengthening of the link between classroom instruction and practice.

A fourth action research tool useful in addressing this pillar is the Grit Scale (Duckworth & Quinn, 2009). This tool, number 16, is especially useful for determining if the school system has facilitated perseverance in students. Scores on this action research tool can be used to create schoolwide initiatives focused on student effort. When students have higher levels of grit, they work harder and longer, and are not as likely to give up. This is an important attribute in a school that focuses on *it's never too late to learn* because teachers need to see that students persevere, even in the presence of challenge.

The final action research tool that we recommend to focus on this pillar relates to the number of students requiring academic recovery at any given time. Action research tool 17 requires an analysis of the percentage of students who need this type of support at a specific point in the year. It also asks for the area of greatest need and the area of least need. One of the things that we have found useful is to observe or interview teachers in the areas of least need to determine if there are actions that can be integrated into the areas of higher need. In addition, the tool requires an analysis of contracts offered to students to determine if there are trends in the needs identified, the supports offered, and if previous contracts have been effective.

Conclusion

In architecture, pillars distribute the weight of a structure and help to hold all of its elements in place. They also ensure that the structure won't collapse under its own weight. A pillar about learning is just as crucial in the mission of a school. When we asked a group of teachers what it would take for their schools to implement this pillar, they identified several things, including

- Really good teaching and reteaching,
- Never giving up on a student,
- Understanding students' lives, and
- Developing strong relationships.

Like the others we have discussed, this pillar is first a philosophy, not a set of procedures. The philosophic agreements must be reached before policy and practice can follow. Otherwise, implementation is haphazard and efforts are likely to fade over time. However, you should expect that teaching, grading, homework, and academic recovery improvements will develop in fits and starts as people experiment and sometimes fail at their early attempts. As with our students, we should allow ourselves the same benefit: it's never too late to learn.

CHAPTER 6

Best School in the Universe

The best school in the universe. "Yeah, right," thinks Mr. Richardson, the veteran 5th grade teacher, who has been in school improvement meetings, work groups, workshops, and conferences for as long as he can remember. "I thought I had heard it all before," he whispers to the teacher to his left. "Now they're even admitting this is all just pie in the sky." Mr. Richardson reopens his newspaper and tunes the facilitator out.

"It's about time we create a positive mission statement," Ms. Southwick stands up and says. "In my educational leadership classes, we've learned about the need to put something out there to really reach for, one that obviously no one really thinks is possible. It's supposed to inspire us, to brand us."

"I've been a football coach in my son's youth league for a long time," Mr. MacKenzie chimes in. "In order to be the best, you have to be well prepared and well equipped, and you have to compete on a level playing field with everyone else. Over 90 percent of our school qualifies for free and reduced lunch, and our kindergartners arrive with oral language skills that are way below developmental milestones. Many of our kids can't express their deepest feelings, let alone use academic language. Until the government and the district level the playing field, it's insulting to be sitting here and talking about the best. We're here in the trenches and working hard and doing the best we can. Let's be realistic. Let's call it what it is. We're treading water and thankful we're not drowning."

Fred Walker, the school's principal, has had enough. The conversation is slipping away from the agenda and back to the same old predictable dialogue and behaviors that have characterized far too many previous staff meetings and workshops. He calmly and in a soft voice begins.

"I was in Ms. Erreca's 4th grade class yesterday. They were writing their own play based on *Riding Freedom* (Ryan, 1999). Two of her students were assisting her in telling the story, discussing its plot and developing its characters. Other students were using graphic organizers to illustrate each character's development and to trace the plot. As they proceeded, Ms. Erreca and the student helpers were soliciting ideas from the class and editing the dialogue to better represent what each character would most likely say. Using think-pair-share, students would read a small section of the developing script, discuss it in small group, and then share their ideas with the whole class. Ms. Erreca used her document camera to show how she was marking their changes to the student script as the discussion proceeded. It was great," Mr. Walker said.

"At one point I saw Ms. Erreca and one of the facilitating students go and sit down next to Kendra, who had been minimally involved in the activity and discussion. Those of you who know Kendra are aware that her life outside school is more complicated than ever and she is really going through a hard time. Ms. Erecca put her hand gently on Kendra's shoulder and whispered, 'Clarisse and I thought you would be perfect for the part of Charlotte.'

"'Me, why?' Kendra responded with suspicion and doubt. 'Well, look at her.' Ms. Erecca borrowed one of the graphic analyzers. 'Here is a girl who has had a lot of challenges in her life. People have called her all kinds of names; they have unfairly judged her and have tried to limit and control her. But she remained strong and principled. She's a strong girl who despite all odds hangs in there and makes it. She reminds me of you, Kendra. You're that girl!'"

Mr. Walker continued. "I saw Kendra sit up a little straighter and her crossed arms opened. 'You can rock it, girl,' said Clarisse. 'Let's read this next section so we can make these lines get real.' Later that day, Ms. Erreca texted me that Kendra had agreed to be cast as Charlotte for their class performance.

"Why do I share this story with you?" asked Mr. Walker. "Because for that moment, in that class, when Kendra opened her arms and engaged, we were the best school in the universe. It wasn't something in the distant future. It had nothing to do with pie in the sky, or rags or riches, or what other schools have or do, or what our achievement was or should be. It was real. It did happen, and for that moment we were the best. I want those moments to occur more often, more noticeably, in more interactions, and in more places across the campus. I want those moments to be our rule and not our notable exceptions. I want to be the best school in the universe. Think long and hard. If you don't want to be or don't think we can be, let's talk, because I am not sure this is the best place for you. But if you want to be the best school in the universe, let's get to work. We have a lot we need to do." Mr. Walker sat down and rolled up his shirtsleeves, a telling gesture.

Mr. Walker got it. And he communicated it. He is prepared to lead his school to be the best in the universe. He knows it's not about competing with other schools for that title. He knows it is a high bar to set for his staff, but he is confident that they can reach it together if they work collectively toward the same mission.

This pillar is not about competing with other schools or striving for external compliance. Nothing says only one school can be the best school in the universe. We want every school to want to be the best, to claim to be the best, and, most of all, to do everything possible to provide the children attending every school the best possible education. Rather than competitive comparisons, this pillar is about internal accountability—creating and holding yourself accountable for being the best we can be and for adopting a system to continuously improve.

Best School in the Universe Pillar

Proclaiming that being the *best school in the universe* is a fundamental pillar of your school makes your efficacy agenda public. Efficacy is defined as the confidence one has in one's ability to reach one's goals. All the goal-setting workshops and meetings are for naught if the group doesn't believe they have what's needed to get there. In a school culture what's needed are the skills to teach and the support to make teaching possible. The mission of being the best school in the universe is not limited to what exists now—it also includes being able to create what is needed. The essential questions for this pillar require a school to ask about what is known, both qualitatively and quantitatively, about the life of the school. Are we the best place to teach and learn? How do we answer this for ourselves? Are we the best place to work? What evidence will we accept of this? Importantly, our definition of the best school in the universe should continue to take form as we know more about where we are and what we are becoming. This requires that we first begin with adopting a reflective perspective to look both within and outside ourselves.

Reflection: The Mirror and the Window

"Why do we use mirrors?" asks Alloway (2010). His answer? "Because our outward appearance is an indicator of our status, professionalism, and credibility. Appearance communicates who we are and what we stand for" (p. 82). Seeing ourselves is powerful. It validates some things and provides us with information about other things that we should adjust. Teachers are encouraged to "take a look in the mirror" regularly. Reflection is a widely recommended practice for improving instruction (e.g., Peña & León, 2011). For example, Snyder (2011), suggests that teachers should reflect regularly on the following:
- Voice level
- Posture
- Eye contact
- Lesson plan sequence
- Pacing
- Classroom management
- Teaching methods
- Error detection
- Age-appropriate materials and pedagogy (p. 59)

Reflection is built into nearly every lesson plan format (Hunter, 1976) because of the widespread acknowledgment that every lesson can be improved upon and that reflecting on a lesson will likely generalize to improvements in other lessons (Grandau, 2005; Sax & Fisher, 2001). We are reminded of an observation that Nancy did of a teacher who requested feedback about the tasks she assigned students. She wanted to know if the tasks were rigorous enough and if students were prepared for the tasks. This teacher, with 18 years of experience, wanted external validation and feedback on areas she could improve. She was not afraid of the conversation she might have with Nancy. She understood the power of reflection as well as the power of interacting about the lesson with another person. When Nancy observed the lesson, she was very impressed. The students were very well prepared for the tasks and they engaged in their group work using language frames. Each student was accountable for his or her participation. During the discussion, Nancy described what she saw and asked the teacher her perspective. The teacher commented, "Yes, I saw all of that, too. But I really wonder if the task was complex enough. I mean, every group seemed to get the answer right. They talked and interacted, but maybe it needed to be more difficult." This led the conversation in another direction, and Nancy commented about the difference between consolidating understanding through practice and collaborating on increasingly complex tasks. There isn't a right answer to this difference, and that isn't our point here. The point is that the teacher's reflection, honest and open, allowed her to go deeper into her teaching and really think about what she wanted for her students.

Reflection is commonly defined as the "rational analytical process through which human beings extract knowledge from their experience" (Jordi, 2011, p. 181). We do it all of the time. Doug reflects on his runs as he walks back home. Nancy reflects on her daily reading of the news on her Kindle. Ian reflects on his interactions with his children as they grow into adulthood. We think about our actions and the reactions of others because it is our nature as thinking beings (e.g., see Abel, 1992).

The more interesting part of the reflecting process, at least to us, relates to the comparisons we use in our reflections. We think of this as the window. Through which window are we looking when we reflect on our own experience? As Jordi (2011) reminds us, "Human beings are forever reconstructing themselves through their experiencing and the movement of their consciousness. Within this process of experiential learning we naturally seek to *make meaning*" (p. 194). In other words, as we reconstruct ourselves, what is the comparison experience we are using? Returning to the work in schools, we often compare ourselves to our peers at the same school. However, *best school in the universe* requires that we expand that window and compare our performance to our dream organization. We have to ask ourselves, "What is the best school I can ever imagine, the school I would want my children to attend, and did we live up to that today?"

Our adoption of this pillar was influenced by our study of and consultation with Baldrige award–winning Sharp HealthCare. In their strategic development of the Sharp Experience, the staff adopted the mission to be the best health care system in the universe. They defined this as being the best place for employees to work, the best place for physicians to practice medicine, and the best place for patients to receive care. That vision became the drumbeat for the core organizational competencies they committed to, their systems to create and reinforce their culture, and the structures they put in place to humanely and effectively exceed their professional responsibilities.

We can live with that. We can even run with that. How can we capture these ideals and translate them into an educational setting? By taking the steps needed to make a school an amazing place to work, teach, and learn. And being the best school in the universe is not only about the future. It is also about creating that environment for today. It is important to highlight the wisdom and depth of Mr. Walker's charge to the staff. He seemed, on the spot, to retell the story of his visit to Ms. Erreca's classroom in a way that operationalized a definition of what the best school means. Each of us needs to examine how to create the conditions necessary to attain the following:

- It is the best place to work.
- It is the best place to teach.
- It is the best place to learn.

The Best Place to Work

Regardless of the type of organization, what is it that creates an excellent workplace? What do employees really value in terms of the time they spend working? Some people say money, but there is evidence to the contrary. Although people do need to earn enough money to live, the amount of money a person makes is not directly correlated with their happiness. In fact, we would argue that money can't buy happiness. We know lawyers and stockbrokers who have higher salaries than anyone in education could ever dream of making, but they are miserable and despise going to work. We also know lawyers and stockbrokers who love going to work.

What we are looking for in creating the best place to work is an organization in which every employee gets up in the morning looking forward to the workday rather than dreading it. When the organization is the best place to work, people enjoy their jobs. What makes people love their job? The answer seems to be meaningful work and making a difference. When employees feel that the work they do matters and that their work is aligned with the organization's mission, work life is better (Studer, 2003). They see that alignment being fine-tuned as they receive support and respect for their work.

In educational language, this is efficacy: the idea that the work you do is meaningful and has an effect. David Lorden (2010), assistant superintendent for the San Diego Unified School District, examined the relationship between the efficacy of students and their teachers, and its effect on student achievement. He argued that if principals could increase individual and collective efficacy in their teachers, then schoolwide achievement increases would follow. What is teacher efficacy? Tschannen-Moran and Woolfolk Hoy (2001) suggest that efficacy clusters into three areas: student engagement, instructional strategies, and classroom management. We will focus on the components of efficacy in the section on the best place to teach that follows. For now, our point is that teachers who have high levels of efficacy like their work better than those who do not. Additionally, people who like their work better are nicer to be around, are more productive, and build the culture of the school. A tool useful in assessing teacher efficacy will be presented at the end of this chapter.

Revisiting pillars. Although we have presented five separate pillars, they do work in concert to create the culture of the school. One of the practices that educational leaders need to use relates to systems for revisiting the pillars. The pillars cannot simply be written down and then posted on a wall.

They have to be talked about, thought about, argued about, and owned. This is directly related to efficacy and employees' need to be part of an organizational mission, knowing how their work complements that mission. When the pillars are revisited, members of the educational community reflect on the implementation and determine how their work, individually and collectively, fits in.

One way to revisit the pillars is through staff retreats. These do not have to be expensive or excessively time-consuming, but they are part of the culture building that needs to occur. As part of the retreat, people need to explore what it means to be successful, what it means to be the best, and whether their school has lived up to the reputation they want. A common starting point for this type of retreat is "Think about the very best school you could ever imagine, maybe even the one you'd like your own children to attend. What does that look like in operation? Does our school reflect that vision?" This conversation starter will result in a thoughtful analysis of each pillar and how they continually improve the educational experience.

Another way to revisit the pillars is to spotlight one pillar at each professional development session. At Johnson Elementary School, the teachers have professional development time every other Friday. Students are released 90 minutes early, thus giving the staff two hours together. As part of each meeting, on a predictable cycle, teachers focus on a specific pillar. How they focus on the pillar changes each time. For example, when they focused on *welcome*, the committee that planned the session provided participants with information from the parent survey (action research tool 5). When they focused on *it's never too late to learn*, the committee that planned the session provided teachers with copies of grading policies and report card forms from area schools so that they could analyze strengths and needs in their own.

Communication. The bane of every organization is communication. It seems that there can never be enough of it and that some people always feel out of the loop. When people feel uninformed, they are less happy at work. They also engage less because they are worried about being redundant. And, perhaps most important, they make mistakes because of their lack of knowledge. We are reminded of a teacher who did not know when grades were due. She submitted her grades the day after they were scheduled to be mailed out. She was frustrated and the administrator was frustrated. On that day, for whatever reason, communication broke down, and the school was not at its best.

The best schools we know of focus relentlessly on communication. They have systems in place to ensure that people have access to information and that they are always encouraged to ask if they are not sure. The systems are all different, yet they result in a level of communication and trust that builds the culture of the school. In one school, they use an electronic calendar to communicate key events with one another. The system they use alerts people when items are added. For example, when the math teacher scheduled a test (competency), it alerted other members of the grade level so that they could schedule their assessments around that one. When a sports event or dance is added, everyone is notified. When a field trip is scheduled, it alerts the team. This calendar is one way to ensure that people have access to information, and it prevents the congestion that can occur when there are conflicting plans.

In another school, the teachers meet every single morning for a 10-minute standing meeting. The focus of their meeting is communication—what do you need to know for today to be a success? Sometimes, seemingly minor events are shared, such as reminding the staff about a track meet. Other times, major events are shared, such as when the staff were informed about the death of the mother of a student. Communication is the focus of this meeting, but something else happens as well. When the adults in a school get to see each other every morning, they build camaraderie. People start to see their peers focused on the same things they are. They start to share stories with one another, stories that build the culture of the school. This morning standing meeting, which takes the place of the after-school staff meeting, provides teachers with a common starting point and signals "We're in this together, and let's go have a great day." And, as you will see in the next section, when communication does not occur effectively, our practice is to close that gap through service recovery.

Service recovery. Even the best-laid plans will not always work. Mistakes are going to happen. We have a service cycle for dealing with these mistakes that will be presented later in this chapter. For now, our attention is on the workplace. When staff members see mistakes being made and nothing being done to correct those mistakes, they start to question their loyalty to, and support of, the workplace. Imagine noticing that there's a problem in the bathroom, perhaps the lack of soap, and reporting that to the head custodian. If that problem is taken care of and is a rare occurrence, it's not going to affect your belief system about your workplace. In fact, if the custodian followed the service cycle described later in this chapter, you might even think, "Hey, this is a great place to work. Not only was the problem taken care of, but the custodian took the time to let me know so." Alternatively, if you notify the custodian weekly about the lack of soap and nothing gets done about it, you start to question the organization as a whole. You probably start thinking, "If they can't even take care of the soap, what else is wrong here?"

Service recovery does not apply only to custodial services. There are times that teachers make mistakes. The important part of service recovery is not disparaging another person or part of the organization in the process of making things right. This is really an important part of the culture that needs to be built. We're all guilty of sanctioning negative discussions about other people or other departments. But let's personalize this experience.

Justin has a bad experience in class. He is angry with the teacher, who he thinks disrespected him. He doesn't want to talk with that teacher. Instead he comes to see you. He describes the situation, and you can see his point. There was probably a little overstepping of bounds. But telling Justin that is not going to build the culture of the school, and it's not going to make him feel any better. Without discounting Justin's experience, you can say, "That's not the Ms. Sweeney that I know. She is really dedicated to student success. Could we go and talk with her together?" This phrasing communicates to Justin that there is another side to the person and that we can work this out. It's also not telling him that he doesn't have the right to feel the way he feels. And it mustn't be a lie. When you provide an alternative perspective about someone, it has to be true. And it has to focus on recovering from the situation, for both the teacher and the student.

This same logic can work in a number of different situations, including miscommunication and conflicts between teachers and teachers, teachers and parents, parents and administrators, students and students, parents and students—just about anyone. The point of having a service recovery focus is to address the problem while maintaining a psychologically healthy workplace. Again, we will provide more information about this in the service cycle section of this chapter.

Celebrations. Another way to ensure that people enjoy their work is through celebrations. These do not have to be major events, but they can be. We are reminded of a BBQ held the first time a local high school, which had been identified as "failing" for several years, made its growth targets. We're also reminded of the daily celebrations of student success and teacher achievements. We've talked about celebrations before, but it is worth repeating. People like their workplaces better when time is devoted to celebrating milestones and achievements.

The Best Place to Teach

When the workplace is great, teachers can focus on teaching. Many of the topics we raised in the previous section relate to teaching, such as teacher efficacy or communication with colleagues. But this aspect of being the best pushes even further. In part, providing teachers the best place to teach means that they have the tools, supplies, and resources necessary to do their job well. Sometimes this means that we have to prioritize our spending so that teachers have the tools they need, including paper, markers, bulbs for their projectors, and enough desks and chairs. Although it is getting harder and harder to meet these needs given the cuts to school system budgets, leaders have to do everything within their power to prioritize providing teachers the tools of the trade. That may mean reaching out to the community for help. Michael Santos, an elementary school principal, attends business partnership meetings every week to inform the business community about his school, the exciting events that are occurring at the school, and what the school needs to be successful. Mr. Santos's school has received computers (true, they were used), pencils, paper, office chairs, and a host of other items from these business partners.

In addition to having the tools necessary to do the job, providing an environment that is the best place to teach means that teachers can focus on teaching and not all of the distractions that typically crowd the mind and schedule of a teacher. It's not that other things get ignored, but rather that it is someone else's job to take care of specific things that are then reported back to teachers. For example, some schools use a paraprofessional to make home visits to encourage student attendance. In other schools, teachers are required to call home to encourage students to come to school. In the former situation, the student or parent had a face-to-face meeting in which attendance is stressed, and that information is communicated to the teacher, who is focused on teaching. That's not to say that teachers shouldn't make home visits, but rather that there is a support system for that aspect of their job. Other distractions that often interfere with teaching, such as logistics for field studies, sporting competitions, special events, and disruptions such as announcements, must be managed.

Providing supplies and managing distractions help ensure that this school is the best place to teach, but they are not sufficient to really operationalize this idea. What is needed is a strong group of teachers who have great efficacy (Tschannen-Moran & Barr, 2004). Teacher efficacy has been defined as "the extent to which the teacher believes that he or she has the capacity to affect student performance" (Berman, McLaughlin, Bass, Pauly, & Zellman, 1977, p. 137). It's different from self-esteem in that it focuses on a specific aspect of a person's life. For example, a person may have low efficacy about cooking or tennis, but still feel pretty good about himself overall. In the previous section, we mentioned the components of teacher efficacy identified by Tschannen-Moran and Woolfolk Hoy (2001). Each of these areas has important considerations for creating a school where teachers know it's the best place to work.

Student engagement. This component relates to the ways in which students engage in school. Importantly, self-efficacy does not consider the actual engagement of students, but rather the beliefs that teachers have related to their ability to engage students. For example, do teachers believe that they can get through to most students? Do they think that they can motivate students to work hard and achieve? Do they think that they have a role in students' critical and creative thinking? When teachers have these beliefs, they enact them in their classrooms. Of course, there might be people who think they can, contrary to the evidence that they can't, but those teachers are few and far between. The evidence on teacher efficacy suggests that teachers who believe that they can do these things—that they have an influence on student engagement—have the results to back up their beliefs (Tschannen-Moran & Hoy, 2007).

Instructional strategies. Like student engagement, this component of teacher efficacy relates to the beliefs that teachers have rather than to their actual implementation. Effective teachers have a host of instructional strategies, routines, and procedures that they can use to improve student learning (Fisher & Frey, 2012). Teachers with high efficacy in this area believe that they can answer students' questions, check for understanding to determine which students comprehended the lesson, differentiate instruction to meet students' needs, and provide additional instruction to those in need. It almost goes without saying that these are important, even critical, areas of a teacher's work. When teachers believe that they can do these things, their students benefit.

Classroom management. Of course, all of the instructional strategies in the world cannot compensate for poor classroom management and structure. Teachers have to use procedures that prevent problematic behavior and address issues as they arise (Frey, 2010). As we have discussed in the chapters on *do no harm* and *choice words*, there are more and less effective ways of doing this. In terms of efficacy, the question is whether the teacher believes that he or she has an influence on student behavior and classroom management. Do teachers think that they make their expectations clear? Do they have systems in place to address student behavior? Do they know how to respond to a disobedient student? As with the other aspects of teacher efficacy, classroom management is directly related to student achievement.

The Best Place to Learn

All kinds of wonderful things happen when students truly feel that their school is the best. Pride and ownership lead to engagement and performance. We frequent two high schools serving the same inner-city community. We have had multiple occasions to interview students from both schools, as well as to observe unstructured interactions and conversations in hallways and common areas. When asked to describe their school, the term *ghetto school* came up frequently at one of the schools and never at the other. Students at one school were more likely to use descriptors that suggested this place was an "alternative to the streets," "a safe place," and "home." The term "ghetto school" was more apt to be described as "it's just school, you know," "it's alright," or "what do you mean?" as if school identity were a nonissue. Certainly kids were kids, and camaraderie and elements of pride existed in both. But it was no surprise that the school that had adopted the pillars advocated in this book provided a sense of place for students. Yes, many of them told us, it was the best school in the universe. And yes, achievement in the two schools, as measured by state accountability tests, is dramatically different.

But being the best requires more than proclaiming it. It requires that a culture be built and maintained and that student achievement be monitored. Schools that monitor student achievement, working to be the best, typically have a data room in which consecutive, previous years worth of student achievement information is analyzed and displayed. Of course, schools that really are the best do not simply post the data—they have conversations about it. It's the analysis of the data, by teachers who are responsible for figuring out what to do based on the data, that really matters. As Thomas (2011) reminds us,

> Data are not best analyzed alone, while you are sitting in front of a computer screen staring at Excel spreadsheets or colorful graphs. Data analyses are most effective when they are performed with other teachers who share the same standards and assessments, and who can discuss concretely and specifically, based on student results, what is working and what is not working to increase student learning in their context. (p. 36)

Creating a system of data analysis has been the focus of many books and articles in education. For example, Boudett, City, and Murnane (2005) suggest eight steps to guide schools in using assessment results to improve student learning:

1. Organize for collaborative work.
2. Build assessment literacy.
3. Create data overview.

4. Dig into student data.
5. Examine instruction.
6. Develop action plan.
7. Plan to assess progress.
8. Act and assess.

In the service cycles section later, we provide more detailed information about using data to create the *best school in the universe*. There is also a data analysis planning sheet included as an action research tool. For now, we'll focus on the improvements made in writing achievement at Brookline Elementary School. When the teachers received the student achievement results and began analyzing performance, they quickly noticed that writing scores were not consistent with students' performance in other areas. In fact, there was quite a gap in students' writing achievement, and that gap was preventing the school from reaching distinguished status.

One of the teachers, in commenting on the data display, said, "It's the way that they test writing. We never know what genre it's going to be or what task students will have."

In response, a colleague said, "That's true, but it is the current measure. We have to figure out how to teach students to write in response to prompts, demonstrating their skills along the way. And this is the real world. We all have to write responses and we don't always get to pick the genre."

Another said, "It makes the 4th grade teachers look bad, but that really is about all of us. We can't teach them to write in one year; it takes longer than that. We should have a plan, a curriculum for writing, that we all agree on. I admit that I don't do much on this because it's not on the 2nd grade assessment. But I would if we all agreed."

This led to the discussion of a writing curriculum, with writing resources, and a lot of professional development sessions, peer coaching, and observations. The teachers committed to changing their students' writing habits and thus their achievement scores. As one of the interventions, they agreed to complete writing screening assessments on each student within the first 15 days of school. In analyzing this data, grade-level groups of teachers met to determine areas of global need and areas of targeted need. The global needs, meaning that at least 75 percent of the students at that grade level needed instruction in a specific area, were the focus of interactions with the peer coach and future grade-level meetings. The targeted needs were addressed through small-group instruction.

The teachers and administrators stayed focused on their goal, discussing writing achievement and writing instruction in all of their professional learning community meetings. They did not take on other initiatives. When the student achievement results were released, writing achievement had increased from 20 percent proficient to 34 percent proficient. In analyzing these results, they realized that they had made those gains without sacrificing achievement in other areas.

During the initial data analysis meeting the following year, one of the teachers said, "Well, with just that little effort, our students scored way better, and their reading, math, and science scores remained high. Just think what we could do if we really tried!"

That comment resulted in a commitment to focus on writing instruction for at least another year. Again, the teachers analyzed screening assessments and determined instructional plans based on student performance. They also agreed to a number of benchmark and progress-monitoring assessments so that they could continue to meet and discuss student progress. Along the way, they began to write their own curriculum and share units of study with one another during their professional learning community time. As one of the teachers commented, late in the second year of implementation, "So this is what a PLC is supposed to feel like. Now I get it. We share resources and we focus on student learning. No harm, no foul. I like it."

Achievement increased again the following year and further convinced the teachers that they were on the right track. They recommitted to the focus for the year and engaged in additional coaching, professional development, and professional learning communities. They shared ideas and success stories, and worried together about individual students who continued to struggle. When the assessment results were released the following year, after three years of implementation, 86 percent of the students were proficient in the area of writing. And what's even more interesting is that math, reading, and science scores increased as well. As the peer coach noted, "I should have guessed that writing improvement would also result in reading improvement, but we also did a lot better on math and science. It's like we have their attention—our students are really doing school now, and it shows."

Organizational Principles

A school that strives to be the best school in the universe is clear on the organizational principles that guide its policies and procedures. These principles serve as an organization's internal guideposts for mapping a course of continuous improvement and culture building:

1. *Being the best school in the universe is not about comparing ourselves to others. It is not boastful or bragging. It is about figuring out what our best is, and then pursuing it relentlessly.*

2. *Being our best is not a condition that is obtained somewhere in the distant future. The time to begin is today.*

3. *In order to be the best school in the universe, we must focus on our reason for being. Our business is education, and our goal is to remove any obstacles that interfere with our reason for being.*

4. *We must attend to the needs of the adults in the organization as carefully as we attend to our students' needs. That means we collectively own our mistakes and fix them, we look each other in the eye every day, and we celebrate our successes.*

5. *We must instill a sense of urgency by ensuring that we make data-driven decisions to understand our students' learning. We will not allow ourselves to be driven to distraction in that effort.*

While these principles serve to guide our work, they are not yet operationalized. The language of process becomes actionable when we articulate service cycles. These cycles allow us to examine how a pillar becomes reality through our daily work.

Putting Principles into Action with Service Cycles

The purpose of service cycles is to give us a script of sorts to follow in order to make the things that we say are important to us a reality. Few things are more frustrating than taking the time to identify our goals and then failing to do anything with them. As one friend of ours in the field of addiction medicine has said many times, "If you can't keep promises you've made to yourself, then what good is your word to anyone else?" Service cycles are a way of keeping a school's promises it has made to itself.

Service recovery. It is not realistic to believe that any organization can operate under the assumption of perfection. Mistakes happen, and they occur regularly. This is especially true when it comes to the messy business of human services. We shouldn't set ourselves up for disappointment by developing a plan of action that leaves no margin for error. The first misstep and the whole structure collapses under the weight of its own discouragement. Building a plan requires building a plan for when it goes awry.

Service recovery is the practice of owning a mistake (even if it's not your doing), fixing the mistake (even if it's not your job), and following up (even if it's not in your job description). The concept comes to us from the field of customer service. If you have customers, you have complaints. But the complaint presents an opportunity for an organization to convert customer dissatisfaction into customer loyalty. In schools, our customers include our students, their families, the community they live in, and even ourselves. The service cycle we have adopted is one developed by Sharp HealthCare (2007). Although our businesses are very different, mistakes and their fallout are universal.

- Apologize.
- Correct the situation.
- Track.
- Take action.

The service recovery principles were in evidence the day Ms. Saldana stormed into the front office of her daughter's middle school. For the fourth time in as many weeks, the school bus has failed to arrive, and she has had to drive her daughter to school. Ms. Saldana is angry because it makes her late for her own job, and she is aggravated that a service that should be reliable has been anything but. The first person she encountered was Alba Edwards, stationed at the front desk. Ms. Edwards listened to the parent's complaint, and even though she had no direct relationship with the transportation department, she apologized to the parent and told her that the problem needed to be corrected immediately. In the meantime, special education director Tonya Burton overheard the raised voice of Ms. Saldana and came out to the waiting area.

"I'm so sorry that happened, Ms. Saldana. You should be able to count on the bus arriving," Ms. Burton said. "I know they work hard in the transportation department, and they would be disappointed to hear about your experiences. They take pride in what they do. I'm going to get in contact with them now so we can solve this together," she said. "I know you need to go to work, so I'll take over and I'll follow up with you later today."

Ms. Saldana's demeanor changed immediately. Although the situation wasn't yet resolved, she was reassured for now that someone else was involved. After exchanging contact information, the women parted. Ms. Edwards and Ms. Burton now turned to one another. "Let me investigate who you'd best talk to about correcting this," Ms. Edwards said. "I'll send you that info as soon as I have it." A few minutes later, the name and phone number of the transportation supervisor for the route appeared on Ms. Burton's computer screen. Ms. Burton explained what had occurred to Arthur Perry in Transportation. Mr. Perry checked the logs and found out that a substitute driver operated the bus for the past couple of Thursdays while the regular driver went to physical therapy. Mr. Perry realized that the route directions for the substitute omitted the stop that Ms. Saldana's daughter used. Within 15 minutes, Mr. Perry had corrected the substitute driver's bus route directions and sent an email to Ms. Burton and Ms. Saldana explaining what had occurred and the steps he had taken to correct it. "If you have any more difficulties, please contact me so I can follow up," he said in the email and included his telephone number. Ms. Burton also placed a call to Ms. Saldana. "Again, I'm sorry this happened, but I'm glad we had the opportunity to correct this. You brought something to our attention that we didn't know about, and it probably was affecting other students as well," Ms. Burton said. Later, Ms. Saldana said, "I'm so used to having to be loud in order to be heard. It was a relief that everything got fixed so easily." Ms. Burton also commented, "In the past I would have wasted time telling Mr. Perry what a problem this was for me. By focusing on service recovery, I can skip all of that."

Rounding. Nothing is better for getting a sense of how the school is running than talking with students, teachers, noninstructional staff, and families during the course of the day. We've informally heard this as "management by walking around," and the practice of doing so can be quite useful for gathering information and building relationships. However, the random nature of this informal practice has always been troubling because it relies on the sudden availability of free time—something no one ever seems to have. This may be due in part to the mistaken notion that this isn't as important as completing a report or following up on messages. We disagree, but we were never quite sure about an alternative.

We were introduced to the concept of rounding through our partnership with Sharp HealthCare. Unlike the walking-around model, rounds are planned and purposeful. They occur daily, and those who do it keep a written log so they can follow up, identify patterns, and gain insight into their own learning. Rounding involves identifying members of a target group and talking with each of them to find out what their experiences have been, what they need, and what they are finding satisfying. For instance, during the first weeks of school, each of us conducts rounds with every classroom teacher. Many of the results are mundane—one teacher needs an extra chair to accommodate a larger class; the air conditioning in another person's room is much too cold. But this practice allows us to resolve problems right away, allowing the teacher to teach.

Another purpose for rounding is to find out what is working so that it can be celebrated and recognized. Talking with students to find out their perspectives is essential. For instance, when we have a new student enroll, we round with that child every day during their first weeks. We ask them why they chose the school, find out how things are going for them, or whether there is anything they need. When they mention another student or adult in a positive way, we probe further to determine why it was meaningful to them. We then follow up with the person mentioned and relay how his or her actions made someone else's day. And we always remember to thank them.

A written log of rounds might seem excessive at first, but it allows us to follow up when a problem can't be resolved right away, or to thank someone when we can't locate her immediately. Most important, rounding logs give us the data to notice patterns that might otherwise go undetected. By examining these logs, we have discovered that there weren't enough recycling containers in public areas of the school, an issue that was resolved by a student who built ones for us as part of his Eagle Scout project. We learned that access to healthy snack choices was a problem, one that was solved by a vice principal who arranged to have a healthy snacks vending machine installed. While these improvements seem small, they empower stakeholders who see that their concerns have been heard.

Studer (2003) considers rounding to be an opportunity to "re-recruit" the people in an organization (p. 93). Whether in your classroom or as a school leader, the people we spend our days with deserve the chance to voice their concerns, share their victories, and see how their presence has an impact on an environment. Our suggested service cycle for rounding is adapted from the Studer Group's (2005) suggestions about these steps:

- Identify a target group for your round (7th grade teachers, newly enrolled students, etc.).
- Make a personal connection and refer to something that person told you in a previous round (if applicable).
- Ask questions about how things are going for them today, whether there is something they need, and if there is someone that should be recognized for their efforts.
- Invite them to tell you what they feel you should be doing more (or less) of.
- Keep a log of your rounds so you can follow up.

Fourth grade teacher Hillary Jenkins conducts rounds within her own classroom to be more responsive. While she confers with students nearly every day about their academic performance, she has begun adding what she calls "The Mighty Five" to these individual meetings. She asks each student "How's your day?" and "Is there anything you need?" She says, "Tell me about a way someone helped you today?" and follows it with "How did you give someone else help?" She finishes each conference with one more question: "What do you want to tell me that I haven't asked?" to prompt more open-ended responses.

"I'm amazed at how they answer that last question," Ms. Jenkins said. "I've gotten such good ideas from them. One student said it would be great to put out a bowl of any uneaten fruit from their breakfast so that they could snack on it midmorning," she said. "Another time, a student told me about how my stern conversation with another student the previous day made her feel. It was great for us to talk about that." Ms. Jenkins's experience reminds us that rounding can happen even among smaller groups, as well as across the entire school. The commitment to dialogue with others is a powerful one for all who are involved.

Making time for data analysis. Few would argue that data analysis has become an essential part of the school improvement process, but in reality it is reserved for infrequent, albeit massive, meeting sessions. These occurrences may be driven by other reasons, such as for accreditation or to meet the deadline for a district-mandated annual school improvement plan. While these are worthy of attention, they are less than useful if data analysis is sporadic. In addition, they become separated from the decisions that are made within a school. In order to make the most of these processes, data analysis and decision making need to be woven into the daily existence of school.

As humans, we analyze data constantly to look for the patterns in our lives. But when it comes to school, mention of the term "data analysis" can cause some to recoil. Don't you need a degree in statistics to do that? The action research tools in this book are a means for collecting data for developing a culture of achievement, and each is worthy of discussion. Now consider the times and places where the adults in the school are together. These places might include the cafeteria or the staff development room. If your school is using a standing morning meeting, it's there. These are ideal locations for establishing a data room. This is a place in the school where pertinent data are displayed so that they can be easily consulted. They might include 90-day attendance trends, standardized test scores for significant subgroups, results of student focus group conversations, or last spring's online family survey. Unfortunately, in some schools these data displays are not fully exploited. Instead, they are located in an out-of-the-way place like a guidance counselor's office. This means that people have to travel there, usually in a small group, in order to view it.

Instead, we encourage schools to locate these data walls in conspicuous places. We have one on the wall of the lunchroom so that students can see it, because they notice patterns we might not otherwise see. Some schools put them in the school library because that's where professional development events occur. What's vital is to identify the places where groups gather to make decisions so that they can consult the data while doing so.

Another essential element of data analysis is making time for it to happen on a regular basis. "Spotlight on Data" can be added as a standing item on every faculty meeting agenda, with different teachers and administrators charged with sharing something with the larger group in five minutes or less. A teacher can share the results of a grade level's student survey on the new algebra curriculum one week, while the assistant principal can show the attendance figures for the Family Literacy Night at the school the next. Provide the staff with a steady data diet to build their collective capacity for assimilating it into daily lives. Here is a suggested service cycle for making time for data analysis:

- Establish a space in the school to create a data room. This place should be as public as possible so that students, teachers, noninstructional staff, families, and visitors can see it.
- Create a "Spotlight on Data" standing agenda item for all faculty meetings.
- When engaged in discussions about school policies and procedures, ask the group to spend several minutes silently consulting the data on display in the room before continuing.
- Ask the group, "Is this decision consistent with what our data are telling us?"
- Reference how you use data in making individual decisions, to model the ways it informs your thinking.

Middle school attendance clerk Roslyn Valdes came up with a plan for displaying attendance data. "I can see the patterns that happen when attendance rises or falls. Is there bad weather? Was a field trip planned? But I'm not sure that others did. So I proposed that we post the attendance data from the previous day by grade level at the top of the stairs where all the students pass," she said. "We used to post notices of meetings for clubs and things like that. So I took all of those down, and now the first thing each morning I put up yesterday's attendance."

Before long, Ms. Valdes's daily attendance bulletin board began seeping into classroom and professional development conversations. One teacher reported that her students noticed that attendance surged on a day when there was an English competency scheduled, but it dipped on another day that week when they knew that two of the teachers would be away for a conference. "They didn't see much point in coming that day, and since it was raining, that was enough to cause a lot of them to take the day off," she said. "I realized that scheduling my competency on a day when some other colleagues would be out would be a way to counteract the 'It's just a sub today' syndrome." Her plan was confirmed a few weeks later when a similar day occurred. "No dip!" the teacher reported.

Action Research Tools

A number of tools are useful in looking, thinking, and taking action that influence the factors that relate to the best school. There is no rubric on what it means to be the best, but there are tools that help determine where work needs to be done to make improvements in the system. The first tool for this pillar relates to teacher efficacy. This tool, number 18, provides information about teachers' efficacy in the three areas identified by Tschannen-Moran and Woolfolk Hoy (2001). We have found this tool especially useful in determining the collective efficacy of the school. By aggregating the survey results, you can determine which areas are in greatest need overall, and this information can guide professional development, coaching, and individual interactions that leaders have with teachers. We have also used this tool in private conversations with teachers to discuss areas in which they would like to focus their own professional development.

We have found action research tool 19 useful in the planning of school improvement efforts. This tool is based on the work done by the Maryland Department of Education and its school improvement efforts. It's a fairly systematic approach to examining data, looking for areas of concern, determining causes for those concerns, developing plans to address those concerns, and then monitoring the impact of the efforts. This process approach to making data work for you is important in the overall quest to be the best school in the universe. We use this in conjunction with the tools that White (2011) provides, which are designed to help people see the patterns in their data.

On his website, Wayne K. Hoy provides a survey that can be used to assess the overall climate of a school (www.waynekhoy.com). We have found this tool very useful in assessing the culture of the school and identifying areas of need. As Hoy, Tarter, and Kottkamp (1991) note, "Organizational culture is a system of shared orientations that hold the unit together and give it a distinctive identity" (p. 5). The tool they developed helps us assess that culture.

The results of these tools should be added to your SWOT analysis that you started in chapter 1. As we noted then, the strengths, weaknesses, opportunities, and threats document should be updated regularly, as new information is obtained and as action plans have effects. The SWOT tool should guide your overall improvement efforts and allow you to focus on the areas of need to improve student achievement.

Conclusion

Being the best school in the universe is not something in the future. It is something that is likely to happen all the time, in all kinds of schools and places. Think about it—in any given moment, in every school, thousands of intentional and unplanned lessons are being taught, and thousands of intentional and unplanned things are being learned. Thousands of interactions are occurring simultaneously between adults and adults, adults and students, and students and students. In any given moment of the school day, a lot is happening—good, bad, ordinary, and extraordinary. The fact is, there are times in the day when we really don't know if it could have gone better. There was a mixture of competence in which the teaching, counseling, and empathy of some led to amazing learning, development, growth, and productivity in another. For that moment, the stars aligned and we were the best in the universe.

The trouble is, a moment later, something undoubtedly happens in which our actions fall short, and the result is that someone comes to believe he is less important, less capable, less worthy than he had felt moments before. In order to be the best, we have to acknowledge the fact that there are times we really miss the mark, and at those times we are no better than the worst school in the universe. It's times like that when we must look again, think some more, and act more responsibly. As Mr. Walker said, our goal, commitment, and expectation is to learn to be the best more often, to make being the best part of the fabric of who we are and what we are committed to achieving. The pillars, the organizational principles, and development of a passionate and competent staff are all investments in a culture proclaiming our collective efficacy.

CHAPTER 7

Enacting the Culture
of Achievement

Creating a school's culture and cultural identity does not happen overnight. It isn't simply the result of a productive or creative retreat. An effective leadership team understands the organization's mission and then spends every moment trying to close gaps that exist between what we say we expect to be with who we actually are. The hard work begins after the exciting, creative, and inspirational mission is proclaimed.

Collins and Porras (1998) discussed how quickly the inspiration of a leader's words becomes meaningless rhetoric when the leader's actions are not consistent with the words. They suggested 1 percent of the work is stating the mission and 99 percent is living it. Too often, the attempt to reinforce the branding of the organization takes more resources than changes in performance. In that case, not much changes.

Kent Peterson refers to this misalignment between vision and performance as "behavioral drift." As depicted in figure 7.1, Peterson suggests it's a matter of reliability, character, and authenticity. He suggests leaders and the organizations they lead state their beliefs (I say...). In turn, each leader acts (I do...). Then each leader's performance has results (I value...). To prevent behavioral drift, Peterson suggests that leaders analyze the alignment of what they say with what they do. This is our *reliability*. Next, he suggests that we analyze what we do and the results or consequences of those actions. This is our *character*. And he recommends that leaders analyze the alignment between the actual results and what we say. This is our *authenticity*.

FIGURE 7.1
Behavioral Drift Model

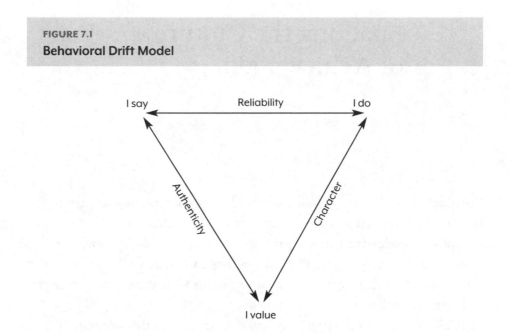

Source: From *Resilient School Leaders: Strategies for Turning Adversity into Achievement* (p. 66) by J. L. Patterson and P. Kelleher, 2005. Alexandria, VA: ASCD. Reprinted with permission.

There is a general understanding that roughly 80 percent of the effects come from 20 percent of the cause. Known as the "Pareto principle" in business (Juran, 1970), this rule is sometimes misunderstood in education. It seems that many school systems put 80 percent of the effort into developing and selling the idea, and 20 percent of the effort into putting the ideas into practice. Of course, there is always a new idea around the corner, which then garners 80 percent of the effort, never leaving any time for implementation. The result is the vast number of educational reforms that have become known as "the flavor of the month," because educators jump into new ideas before fully committing to ones they have already developed.

We are not suggesting that educators keep riding a dead horse. On the contrary, our advocacy for action research and dynamic improvement cycles is an indication that we think schools can improve through systemic change. Having said that, we do believe that it is important to realize that once a focus is committed to, the hard work begins.

The point is worth repeating: culture does not happen overnight or by proclamation. It happens as a community develops history and the *beliefs, values, rituals, ceremonies, stories, and physical symbols* (Collins & Porras, 1998) that accumulate as a part of that history. A culture will be created in your school either purposefully or by chance. That culture will affect the overall performance and effectiveness of the school. To purposefully develop a school-wide culture that supports and drives the effectiveness of your academic press takes thoughtful and reflective perseverance, and that takes strong leadership.

Change Is Fragile

There is a fundamental theorem observable in the physical, natural, and organizational sciences. Simply stated, there is a *natural tendency for systems to regress to the mean* (Galton, 1886; Samuels, 1991). That regression happens for all kinds of reasons. Jack has been a middle school science teacher at his school for nine years. Truth be known, he is quite passive-aggressive when it comes to change. He believes status quo is the school's organizational reality. He has "seen it all before" when people come in with new ideas, new initiatives, new programs, and new energy. He sits back and watches the fanfare, and he truly believes that the attention will wane, resources will dwindle, and leaders will leave or become distracted by reality. Time and time again he has seen things will go back to the way things were. *Regression to the mean.*

In fact, next time he knows some more of his peers will share his cynicism. The culture of his school has suffered from the aforementioned 80:20

rule. Jorge is also a veteran teacher, but he embraced and actively participated in developing new service cycles in which restorative practice would replace the school's previous consequence-driven discipline plan. However, when a student disrespected Jorge in front of his class, he demanded severe punishment instead of applying the newly adopted restorative practices. In other words, innovations were exciting in principle, but when confronted with real time and personalized problems, the old ways seemed most appropriate. *Regression to the mean*.

Delta High School received grant support to change grading procedures such that students received incompletes instead of *D*s and *F*s. The grant was used to provide an exciting and robust after-school program that served as the main strategy for helping students clear their incompletes with passing grades while learning more content. When the grant ended, so did the extra funds used to operate the after-school program. The school curriculum committee determined that without that program, the ability to support students to clear their incompletes was lost, and *D*s and *F*s once again became options for teachers to use. The *never too late to learn* pillar began to crumble. *Regression to the mean*.

Rolling out a reform effort takes tremendous leadership skills, particularly if the reform effort is designed to fundamentally change teaching behaviors, mentoring relationships, and culture. It takes competent leaders to create consensus regarding a need to develop a reform agenda, to make the development of the reform efforts an inclusive effort among stakeholders, and to construct a plan based on best and emerging practices with stakeholder buy-in. There will be resistance and barriers at each turn. Many leadership teams never make it to blast-off, and the forces of inertia inherent in the status quo end the momentum of reform. But skillful leadership teams can develop and articulate an agreed-upon reform agenda. The reports get filed, the newsletters get written, the staff development occurs, the plan becomes public at open house and on the school board agenda, and momentum interrupts the status quo. If you think this means the mission is accomplished, your reform agenda may not last any longer than the new restaurant that advertised one thing and delivered another. The skillful leadership team, however, understands that the school has committed to a focus, and that focus will be their responsibility to manage and lead. In the early stages of implementation, the investment in staff and the public communication of what is being done and why is a conscious undertaking. The leadership team will engage in constant gap analysis and adjust supports and engage in service recovery to close performance gaps.

Leadership: Will and Skill

This whole process described thus far, which is not nearly as linear and uninterrupted as we have described it, takes incredible leadership will and skill. But the hard work is still in front of you, *because the process of changing practice and developing culture is fragile.* Attention slips, awareness wanes, new people come, founders leave, resources dwindle and get directed elsewhere, crises occur, public priorities are redirected by politics, world events engage us, new discoveries and ideas appeal to us—and then there is the press. If the leadership team does not stay on message, there will be a regression to the mean, and the change that was once a vision will now be unauthentic rhetoric. As you commit to a conscious development of your school's culture, please realize it will be your job every day to assess what is going on, to reflect on how to close the gaps and enhance performance that builds that culture, and to lead a dynamic process of ongoing reform and revitalization. Do not take the complexities of this effort for granted, or its fragility will set you back. However, it is our belief that we do not have a choice. It is our responsibility to purposefully and continually assess and develop the culture of our school.

"If it's lonely at the top, there is something you are not doing right." In that simple statement, Maxwell (2008) challenges the belief that leadership is conducted by the organization's leader, whether it be the CEO or the principal. We do not begin to take for granted that the principal's job is a 24/7 commitment and the responsibilities assumed and decisions made are complex and can affect many lives and the success or failure of the school. But an effective leader of an organization takes time to build a leadership team that allows for an effective orchestration of the school's financial, operational, and programmatic performance. And that leadership team builds the capacity of more stakeholders throughout the organization to assume various leadership roles and responsibilities. The leadership team reduces the "lonely at the top" stereotype and creates greater capacity to look, think, and act upon the gaps that exist between vision and performance. The leadership team orchestrates ways to effectively engage, empower, and involve others in the school's action research agenda. The team is a safe place to sound ideas and concerns, a place to ask for and offer help, and a place to complement the strengths of others with your own. The business of developing and changing a school's culture requires a leader, with the support of his or her leadership team, making the process transparent and inclusive. Otherwise, school culture will remain the hidden curriculum instead of a process that is a community agenda that can be assessed for its reliability, character, and authenticity.

The role of the leadership team requires that they *model the way*. The mission, the pillars, the organizing principles, the service cycles, and the action research program improvement cycles must clearly define the behavior of each member of the leadership team. If you are too busy for that, your staff will soon find other priorities to occupy their physical time and intellectual reflections.

However, the most important aspect of building capacity for our cultural identity and maturity is in the development of the entire staff, from principal to teacher to support staff to volunteers. The development of a passionate and competent staff is the school's most significant, precious, and strategic resource. The leadership team must see the development of its entire staff as one of its highest responsibilities. This includes the following:

1. *Hiring policies and practices.* The mission of the school, its academic press, and its cultural pillars must be discussed as part of the hiring process. Successful candidates should be screened and interviewed with these factors in mind, and accepting a job offer should include the candidate's understanding and commitment to supporting each.

2. *Staff feedback and evaluations.* Regular discussions with staff should allow each member of the leadership team to provide feedback on what is going well and areas in which they would like information, support, or change. Follow-up from leadership team members regarding information collected during these informal discussions demonstrates

respect to staff for their opinions and the power they have to engage and own the development of school culture. In addition, staff members are provided written and verbal feedback after walkthroughs or specific interactions about ways in which they are, or might better, support the school's cultural pillars. Finally, performance related to each pillar is a part of each staff member's formal evaluation such that staff know it is a priority and there can be a constructive discussion regarding strengths, goals, and support needs. These are also times in which a realistic discussion regarding whether this school and its commitment to its cultural pillars is a place the staff member feels in sync with and ultimately whether this assignment is the best match for his or her talents and beliefs. Crucial conversations are among the most difficult and important aspects of building culture in schools.

3. *Daily standing meetings.* Every Ritz-Carlton property has a daily meeting in which staff recommit to their core values and customer service practices. As part of this conversation, they examine their successes. Schools can do the same thing. Rather than a bimonthly staff meeting for 90 to 120 minutes, imagine having 10 minutes of time together every morning. At our school, the daily standing meeting occurs each and every morning. This meeting quickly gets everyone on the same page for the day. This is part of what Deal and Peterson (2009) call living logos, or culture building through the symbolism in daily routines. What we have heard over and over from schools that have implemented this practice is fascinating. We've frequently heard variations on the same thing: "Good teachers have always bonded with their students; now they are bonding with their colleagues as well." The difference with standing meetings is frequency of contact, not duration. There is also a difference in participation. In most staff meetings, some people are grading papers, others are on their computers, and some are attending to the discussion at hand. When the faculty stand around in a circle, in the same room together, they engage more often. In addition to updates about the day, the standing meeting can be used to spotlight student success and needs. They can also be used to build culture through symbolic gestures and celebrations, such as

acknowledging births and birthdays or asking one person each day to make closing comments before saying, "Go, team!"

4. *Staff recognition, respect, and celebration.* We think it is critical that staff are treated and recognized for being well prepared, dedicated, and committed professionals. We believe back-to-school meetings should have some class. We like to pick a nice place, provide a good meal, give them an agenda that will be simulating and culture building. We also think it's important to take time during the year to have holiday, happy hour, and end-of-the-year celebrations that are fun, bonding, and reinforcing of the work, students, and camaraderie. Furthermore, we think that accomplishments should be shared and celebrated, as when a teacher came back to work following radiation or when a paraprofessional earned his bachelor's degree. We have already discussed the importance of choice words with students; the same holds for our interactions with teachers. The language we use should be respectful and attribute success to them. It should build their identity and agency, and every adult in the school should feel welcome and valued. We have adopted Sharp HealthCare's "attitude of gratitude" practices by regularly sending handwritten notes home to each other, our staff, and our stakeholders. We have affirmed how much more special, heartfelt, and meaningful receiving a handwritten note in the mail is than an email. Notes are regularly sent to recognize how an incident was handled, how a project was completed, or the impact of a contribution of time, effort, or money.

5. *Staff development.* This is the item that must be most carefully designed and executed. This is where the seeds of a school's investment in culture and its academic press are designed and turned into commitment, passion, and competence. In fact, this is the crux of leadership—developing others. Although it may be easier to do a lot of things yourself, you can't do them all, and it's not in the best interest of the organization if you try. We have to share responsibility with our coworkers and provide them all with the support they need to reach the next level of performance. As such, we choose to devote considerable attention to this area.

Investing in Human Resources

A culture committed to student learning must be equally committed to the learning of teachers. An environment that provides thoughtful support for the younger people in the building would ultimately not be able to sustain its efforts without nurturing the adults as well. A tremendous cultural shift is required if educators are to truly see themselves as lifelong learners. This means tearing down the hierarchical barriers that foster complacency and stifle excellence.

A major barrier is that many educators view professional development and coaching in a negative light. After-school professional development is seen as encroaching on "my" time, rather than as a part of the work of school. In some schools, professional development time is perceived as a good time to schedule nonwork appointments: the dentist and the auto mechanic seem to get more attention than the colleagues who have organized the meeting. The absence of members of the community diminishes the value of the community, as those who dutifully attend feel resentful and unable to make decisions without full participation. Others may attend in body but not spirit. They grade papers, check their cell phones, and watch the hands of the clock as they move slowly onward.

Teacher observations are also mutually dreaded. Teachers may see it as a once- or twice-a-year event to be endured, while administrators are focused on moving through the to-do list of too many staff. Neither is particularly attuned to the opportunity to hold a conversation with one another about the most important thing a school does: teach. Instead, there are forms to be completed, signed, and filed away.

Coaching has perhaps the strongest negative reputation of all. Beyond supporting beginning teachers for the first year or two in the profession, the presence of an instructional coach in the room is viewed with suspicion. After all, why would a coach be there unless the teacher wasn't doing a good job? And by the way, who sent you? Is all of this going to be reported to the principal? Although concerns about professional development, teacher observations, and coaching are rarely voiced in a large group, they are fodder for discussion in small ones. But in a culture that truly believes that it's never too late to learn, these practices could look quite different.

Professional Development

A major criticism of conventional professional development is that it is disconnected from the classroom experience, and it is thought of as a series of discrete events on a calendar, rather than an ongoing process that occurs throughout one's career (Webster-Wright, 2009). This perception is reinforced by contractual and state licensing mandates that require teachers to log hours in formal professional development events. However, even within these parameters, professional development events can be made more or less useful according to their design. Professional development that is most useful will do the following:

- Foster ownership and build capacity by giving teachers an active role in determining the focus of professional development, as well as its design and implementation (Fullan & St. Germain, 2006)
- Build skills through purposeful transfer of learning from training to classroom practice (Joyce & Showers, 2002)
- Monitor progress in order to make necessary changes throughout the process (Guskey, 2000)
- Create communities of learners to sustain efforts long-term (Borko, 2004)

The unique logistical demands of a school make extended discussion of schedules difficult in this space, but there is merit in considering ways in which professional development can be delivered while adhering to these principles. They include school day professional development, coaching corners, and professional learning communities.

School day professional development

Conventional professional development wisdom places these events after the students have left for the day—precisely when teachers are losing steam. We worked with a high school for a number of years that used prep periods for professional development, allowing teachers to participate earlier in the day. The school used a 4×4 block schedule for students, allowing each teacher a daily 90-minute prep period (Canady & Retting, 1995). Twice a month, teachers gathered for professional development, which was repeated four times throughout the day. By the end of the fourth period, all teachers had attended. The format varied, including presentations of information, small-group discussion and planning, and schoolwide book clubs (Fisher, Everlove, & Frey, 2009). Another benefit was that this large staff of 125 could work in smaller cross-disciplinary communities of 30 or so, allowing for more personalized and meaningful experiences within and outside the meeting. Repeating professional development four times in a day shifts the burden to the professional development staff, but the reward is in designing events that are cognizant of teachers' workloads and the need to participate in more cohesive groups.

Coaching corners

Another innovation we have used in many schools is coaching corners (Fisher & Frey, 2006). The purpose of coaching corners is to promote transfer of learning by bridging the divide between discrete professional development events and classroom practice. Teachers volunteer (or are recruited and encouraged to volunteer) to provide a short demonstration lesson and discussion for four peers. Prior to the coaching corner event, teachers sign up for three or four demonstration lessons, building their own unique schedule. The topics are varied, and teachers can choose to participate in coaching corners within or across grade levels or disciplines. Keeping the groups small reduces the anxiety that many teachers feel in presenting in front of their peers, and strategic recruitment efforts ensure that varying levels of experience and expertise are represented at each event. We have found that coaching corners events result in teachers visiting each other's classes for further collegial coaching.

Professional learning communities

Many schools have organized into professional learning communities (PLCs) as a means for conducting focused initiatives within the context of mutually aligned small groups (Schmoker, 2006). The work on starting, organizing, and maintaining PLCs is extensive but circles around three major principles:

- PLCs are focused on student learning.
- PLCs use results to make decisions.
- PLCs function best in a collaborative culture (DuFour, 2004).

The research on PLCs should be viewed within the context of the culture of the school. To be sure, there are anecdotes about the misapplication of professional learning communities that have ultimately failed to deliver promised outcomes. But a closer examination of what occurred invariably exposes problems with one of more of these principles. A PLC that is dedicated to topics unrelated to student learning is not going to bring about positive changes in student achievement. While this may seem obvious, you would be surprised to observe many PLCs that function in spheres outside student learning. While their official purpose may be about teaching and learning, the discussions may in fact be focused on departmental logistics, or the PLC's own agenda may be encroached upon by outsiders (Lujan & Day, 2010). Researchers' recommendations are sound: (1) keep PLC time sacred, (2) keep the focus on student learning, (3) make sure new faculty are trained in the PLC process and purposes, and (4) create shared planning time so PLC members can follow up on the work (Lujan & Day, 2010).

Teaching Observations

A second aspect of a culture of learning is observations of teaching. We use this language purposefully; we are not referring to observations of the *teacher*, which are part of the contractual and licensure requirements of the district and state. Instead, we are referring to the practice of observing teaching and learning. This occurs in planned observations among teachers and administrators, as well as in learning walks conducted by teams to calibrate quality indicators. In both of these processes, collaboratively defined "look fors" guide the process. For example, the Sarasota County (FL) Public Schools uses the form found in the appendix (action research tool 14) to conduct classroom walkthroughs. The development of their "look fors" is part of an ongoing process of professional learning. Because their district has been focused on a gradual release of responsibility instructional framework, the teaching observations are similarly aligned. The purpose of the form is not to catalog deficits and shortcomings, but rather to provide a starting point for dialogue. For that reason, administrators and teachers use this document as a record of what they noticed and what they have questions about. The conversations that follow are where the true learning occurs.

School teams are also organized to conduct learning walks to identify and refine quality indicators. Built around the work of City, Elmore, Fiarman, and Teitel (2009), learning walks are used to develop rubrics for quality indicators. Our work in Chula Vista (CA) Elementary School District has centered on the ongoing use of this process to drive professional learning. Led by Assistant Superintendent John Nelson, each of the 44 schools in the district has identified an Instructional Leadership Team (ILT) composed of teachers and a building administrator. Teams identify their purpose in advance, then visit numerous classrooms in their building and neighboring schools to identify patterns of practice. Their learning walks are typically brief (15 minutes or so), and participating teachers know in advance what the team has selected as their purpose. After every third or fourth classroom, the team pauses to discuss what they observed across the classrooms. These observations of pattern are used to build quality indicators and, most important, a rubric of varying levels of implementation. Educators in Chula Vista were adamant about this point. They did not want to create a rubric using the "always/sometimes/never" yardstick, but rather wanted each of the cells to be descriptive so that educators could use these as points of conversation. Because of the deepening understanding of a shared vision of quality, the rubrics are held in draft form to reflect this evolution. A rubric for productive group work, one of Chula Vista's professional development initiatives, can be found in the appendix (action research tool 10).

Coaching

Many professions rely on the advice of a seasoned veteran to continually improve the performance of its members. We're familiar with the role of coaches in professional sports: no team would dream of fielding a team without the presence of specialists who build athletic skills. In start-up companies that have achieved early success but are now stalled, the recruitment of a "gray hair" is seen as a stabilizing force who brings wisdom and experience to the table. But in education, coaches are scarce, save for those who are charged with mentoring novice teachers. It is ironic that a profession predicated on beliefs about the complexity of teaching and learning will turn a distrustful eye toward someone meant to help us get better at doing so. We shouldn't be mouthing the words "lifelong learner" while refusing to be one ourselves.

Disagreements about the role of the coach have contributed to this distrust. We have all heard stories of the misapplication of coaches, such as requiring them to report what they have observed to the principal, using them as floating substitutes in classrooms, and assigning them to duties that reduce the amount of time they can actually coach. In addition, some coaches have been unqualified or have proven to be lacking in the interpersonal and communication skills necessary for this job. But these should be viewed as nonexamples and errors to avoid, not an indictment of an entire segment of the profession.

The fact is that an investment in coaching for all teachers represents a means for facilitating ongoing peer interactions about our practice. Professional development, observations of teaching, and coaching don't exist in silos, distanced from the mission of school and instead marginalized as the business of school. They need to be collectively viewed as the tools and processes used to move closer to the mission. They are tools for fostering interactions, not for subdividing and sorting people. Fullan (2008) describes three conditions necessary for practitioners to engage in these meaningful ways of work:

- When the larger values of the organization and those of the individuals and groups mesh;
- When information and knowledge about effective practices are widely and openly shared; and
- When monitoring mechanisms are in place to detect and address ineffective actions while also identifying and consolidating effective practices. (p. 45)

An instructional coach is the glue that holds together professional development and observations of teaching by finding ways to move forward from discussion to classroom practice. As such, the coach is a valuable member of any organization because he or she helps all of us figure out "the next right thing" to do. In the same way that children can become overwhelmed and paralyzed by the enormity of a task, so can teachers. A skilled coach works in partnership with a teacher to figure out how to put one foot in front of the other. And as educators, we need to recognize that a culture of achievement requires that we maintain a forward motion.

Given the hard economic times that schools are facing, the existence of instructional coaches is threatened. If you are lucky enough to have one or more, celebrate. Then make sure you are maximizing the gifts that an instructional coach brings to an organization. Ensure the sanctity of the coach's role as someone whom teachers can confide in. Just as children need trusted adults, so do the adults in our school. Be sure that his or her day isn't unnecessarily compromised with other unrelated tasks. We recall looking for an instructional coach one day at an elementary school we were working with, only to discover that she was passing out lunches in the cafeteria. Feeding children is important, to be sure, and emergencies do arise. But this woman handed out lunches every day. Using an instructional coach to fill in personnel gaps deflates the morale of the individual and the organization.

The Employment Cycle

> *Sunrise doesn't last all morning, a cloudburst doesn't last all day... All things must pass*—(George Harrison, 1970)

Schools, like any organization, say hello to new team members and good-bye to others each year. A history of too much annual turnover is usually a sign that the organization has systemic problems or that there is an external factor at work such as the impact of a budget crisis forcing the terms of a bargaining agreement. Organizations pride themselves when low turnover is reported, but some amount of turnover is predictable, and some level of turnover is healthy. We remember a colleague who used to lecture on reform through staff attrition. He was quick to add that its effectiveness depended on sound hiring practices. Notwithstanding the fact that people will come and go, managing these processes will directly affect school culture. The duration of one's involvement can vary from less than a day to a long career spanning decades, and the terms and reasons for hiring, staying, and leaving will vary greatly as well.

The orientation of new employees is the beginning of the employment cycle. Earlier in this chapter we alluded to the need for ensuring that responsibilities and commitments to the school's vision and pillars are an overt and implicit aspect of the interview and hiring process. These aspects need to be specified in job descriptions, employee handbooks, and job offers and acceptances. Every new team member then needs to be properly introduced, oriented, and welcomed. When we have made errors in this area in the past, it was in dropping the ball too abruptly and assuming too much. Skillful leaders broker introductions, connections, and collaborations of new employees with other team members. They check in with them regularly, and they spend time helping employees understand and engage in the academic press and cultural development of the school. This cannot be accomplished by simply having the new staff stand up and be introduced at the faculty meeting. Remember that current staff have been developing and living as a part of the school's culture. They have been a part of its history, rituals, successes, and challenges. New employees need to be welcomed into, and made an informed member of, that culture. Effective leadership teams sit down and map the introduction and orientation of each new employee based on the context in which they have been hired and their previous experience and training. We highly recommend that schools purposefully plan their new employee orientation cycles.

We have adopted several employment practices presented by Studer (2003). First, he recommends informally checking in with employees by regularly rounding with new employees. We use prompts like "How is it going? What has been your best experience so far? Is there anything you need to do your job better? Do you think there are things we could do better to be the school we talked about during your interview and orientation?" We try to repeat these same types of questions in scheduled discussions with employees 30, 90, and 120 days into each calendar year. During these scheduled discussions, we not only listen but also provide constructive feedback and observations. We discuss individualizing professional development plans, and we discuss our observations regarding contributions to the academic and cultural agenda of the school.

Studer also suggests that leaders continually evaluate employee performance with respect to the school's academic and cultural standards. In addition to developing a professional development and growth plan, he suggests starting to determine whether an employee is currently a strong performer, a performer who is demonstrating both skills and needs, or an employee whose performance must change dramatically in order to be a productive and contributing member of the team.

Strong performers need regular feedback, assurance, and acknowledgment. We too often take them for granted, but our agenda must be to retain them as passionate and committed members. The second group of employees are developing skills but have yet to become high achievers. Your leadership team must determine, with them, what investments will make them join the ranks of your high achievers. The point is that mediocrity cannot be tolerated long-term, and with support they can become high achievers. The middle-level achievers need to know that the goal is their retention and where they should focus their improvement efforts. If not, they may move into the third group of employees whose performance is yet to be value added.

When an employee's performance overall is not adding value to the core vision, mission, and culture of the school, another cycle needs to be purposefully entered. The cycle should result in helping the employee make adjustments in performance that turn that person into a value-adding member or in determining that employment at your school should be reconsidered. This whole process needs to be transparent, follow due process policies and procedures, and adhere to any bargaining or contractual agreements that are in place. Effective documentation of incidents and examples when performance violated agreed-upon aspects of the school's adopted plans to provide academic rigor and build culture should be kept. Conversations typically advance over time from verbal warnings to written warnings and notices. Crucial conversations must occur, and expectations must be specific and clear, whether provided verbally or in writing.

Some musicians are great soloists but are unable to play in an orchestra or in every band. They are unprepared to be a member; they just want to be a soloist. Some teachers are great teachers but are unwilling to be a part of the instructional plan and cultural structure the school has adopted. When their lack of participation in the school's vision and adopted approaches detracts from schoolwide effectiveness, it is time for a crucial conversation. If they cannot, or will not, align their competence, attitude, and individuality with the schoolwide design, the next crucial conversation has to be about a job match. More teachers have chosen to leave our school by a mutual decision regarding a bad match than by completing the termination process. Otherwise, effective teachers who act in a manner that disrupts the culture you are creating are not effective teachers in your school. Sharp HealthCare advised us that a highly skilled nurse who will not implement Sharp's organizational principles will not be retained despite his or her technical superiority. Our crucial conversations might go something like this: "We think you are a great teacher, but we believe you would be happier and more productive working in a school that values and supports your approach. We have adopted a schoolwide approach that is not well matched to your philosophies and skill sets." The performance gaps might relate to a fundamental difference in grading or disciplinary policies. It might relate to a reluctance to reconsider interactions with stakeholders that are more *welcoming* or use *choice words*. It might relate to teaching approaches that disrupt the habits of mind and academic skills and mindsets that are being otherwise constructed schoolwide. Avoiding crucial conversations or being vague and subtle about performance gaps rarely serve the employee or the organization well. Many employees would simply be happier and more productive elsewhere, and it is the leader's job to see whether the employee, on reflection, agrees.

In any event, members join and members leave. Some leave based on predetermined duration. Some leave for opportunity, advancement, and wanderlust. Some leave for documented cause. Some need to make a career change, and others need to pursue a school in which there is a better match with their skill sets and philosophies. Some depart for tragic and untimely reasons, and others earn their retirement. Our job as leaders is to support and retain our high achievers and develop those with promise. It is also to recognize when employees are not a value-added asset to our mission and to plan and act accordingly. Helping end the cycle of employment in our schools with appropriate transition plans and celebrations is also part of our culture. While you are here you will be welcomed, your development will be supported, and your performance will be respectfully and honestly critiqued. When it's time to say good-bye, we all should and will.

Conclusion

Building the culture of a school takes time and effort. Getting the right people in the right position, and supporting them, is part of the culture-building process. But it's more than that. Culture is created and maintained by all of the members of a community, not simply the formal leaders. Articulating the mission and vision of a school, and working every day to realize that mission and vision, is the responsibility of every member of the school community. We have presented culture building in five areas, including welcome, do no harm, choice words, it's never too late to learn, and best school in the universe. Together, these five ideas, and the host of activities required to enact them, can create an environment that is conducive to learning. As with every other species, we thrive in a hospitable environment. The tools in this book were designed to assess, create, and maintain a hospitable, engaging, and enjoyable environment where administrators, teachers, and students thrive.

ACTION RESEARCH TOOL 1
Self-Analysis Worksheet

While insights gained from external examiners or reviewers are always helpful, you know your organization better than they will. You are currently in an excellent position to identify your organization's key strengths and key opportunities for improvement (OFIs). Having just completed your responses to the Baldrige Criteria questions, you can accelerate your improvement journey by doing a self-analysis of your responses to all seven Criteria categories using this worksheet.

Start by identifying one or two strengths and one or two OFIs for each Criteria category. For those of high importance, establish a goal and a plan of action.

Criteria Category	Importance High, Medium, Low	For High-Importance Areas			
		Stretch (Strength) or Improvement (OFI) Goal	What Action Is Planned?	By When?	Who Is Responsible?
Category 1—Leadership					
Strength					
1.					
2.					
OFI					
1.					
2.					
Category 2—Strategic Planning					
Strength					
1.					
2.					
OFI					
1.					
2.					

ACTION RESEARCH TOOL 1—(*continued*)
Self-Analysis Worksheet

Criteria Category	Importance High, Medium, Low	For High-Importance Areas			
		Stretch (Strength) or Improvement (OFI) Goal	What Action Is Planned?	By When?	Who Is Responsible?
Category 3—Customer Focus					
Strength					
1.					
2.					
OFI					
1.					
2.					
Category 4—Measurement, Analysis, and Knowledge Management					
Strength					
1.					
2.					
OFI					
1.					
2.					
Category 5—Workforce Focus					
Strength					
1.					
2.					
OFI					
1.					
2.					

ACTION RESEARCH TOOL 1—(*continued*)
Self-Analysis Worksheet

Criteria Category	Importance High, Medium, Low	For High-Importance Areas			
		Stretch (Strength) or Improvement (OFI) Goal	What Action Is Planned?	By When?	Who Is Responsible?
Category 6—Operations Focus					
Strength					
1.					
2.					
OFI					
1.					
2.					
Category 7—Results					
Strength					
1.					
2.					
OFI					
1.					
2.					

ACTION RESEARCH TOOL 2
How to Develop a Mission Statement

A mission statement may look simple, but it should communicate the core of your organization with a precise statement of purpose. Words should be chosen for meaning and clarity, not technical jargon.

The mission statement should be about three sentences long and touch upon these key points:

- ❖ Who we are
- ❖ What we do
- ❖ What we stand for
- ❖ Why we do it

According to MindTools (http://www.mindtools.com/pages/article/newLDR_90.htm), to create your mission statement, first identify your organization's "winning idea." This is the idea or approach that will make your organization stand out from its competitors. It is the reason that customers will come to you and not your competitors. Next identify the key measures of your success. Make sure you choose the most important measures (and not too many of them!). Combine your winning idea and success measures into a tangible and measurable goal. Refine the words until you have a concise and precise statement of your mission, which expresses your ideas, measures, and desired result.

ACTION RESEARCH TOOL 3
SWOT Analysis

Threats	Opportunities

Weaknesses	Strengths

ACTION RESEARCH TOOL 4

Secret Shopper Checklist for Enrolling in a New School

Service Cycle Question	YES	NO	Evidence
Were you greeted in a timely fashion?			
Was it a friendly greeting?			
Were you asked how you could be helped?			
When you reported that you might be enrolling a student in the school, were you provided with information and materials on how to do so?			
Were you discouraged from enrolling a child in the school?			
Did you interact with anyone else besides the person at the front desk?			
Were you offered an opportunity to tour the school, either at this time or at a later scheduled time?			
Did someone ask for your contact information so they could follow up with you?			
Were the interactions between students and adults in the front office environment generally positive?			
Please describe the interactions you witnessed.			

ACTION RESEARCH TOOL 5
Family Survey

We would like to know your opinions on how well our school is meeting your family's and child(ren)'s needs and how you feel about your school experience.

There are no right or wrong answers.

We are interested only in your opinions.

Your answers will be kept private. Your answers will be combined with those of other parents in a report of the survey findings.

Your input is very important. Findings of the survey will be summarized and used to improve the school's efforts in strengthening the partnership between parents and the school.

What is/are your child(ren)'s grade level(s)? (circle all that apply)

K   1   2   3   4   5   6   7   8   9   10   11   12

Were any of these children enrolled at our school last year?   ☐ Yes   ☐ No

When you visit the school...	ALL of the time	MOST of the time	SOME of the time	NONE of the time
Is the reception staff friendly and helpful?				
Are the teachers easy to talk to?				
Are the administrators easy to talk to?				
Do you feel welcomed?				

What is/are the best way(s) to communicate with you and/or your family?

(choose all that apply)

☐ School memos (e-mails, website, letters, etc.)

☐ Children's teachers

☐ Counselor

☐ Direct contact (phone call, school/home visit, meeting)

☐ Other—please specify: _____

What else would you like to tell us about communication at our school? _____

_____

ACTION RESEARCH TOOL 5—(*continued*)
Family Survey

Last school year, were you contacted by someone from the school regarding…

(choose all that apply)

☐ Your child's academic success

☐ Your child's academic struggles

☐ Your child's positive social behavior

☐ Your child's negative social behavior

☐ Your child's recognition in achievement (sports, music, volunteerism, etc.)

☐ No reason, just to make contact (say hello, introduce self, etc.)

☐ Other—please specify: _____

What else would you like to tell us about contact regarding your child's successes and difficulties?

_____

_____

How much do you agree or disagree with the following statements?	STRONGLY agree	AGREE	DISAGREE	STRONGLY disagree
The school has high expectations for my child.				
The school clearly communicates those expectations to me and my child(ren).				
My child is learning what he or she needs to know to be successful after graduating.				
My child receives assistance when he or she is having difficulty academically or socially.				
The curriculum and activities keep my child interested and motivated.				
My child is happy at school.				

What else would you like to tell us about learning at our school? _____

_____

Thank you for taking the time to complete this survey. We can't be the Best School in the Universe without families like yours.

ACTION RESEARCH TOOL 6
Student Focus Groups

1. What is the best thing about this school?

2. Can you think of a time when you really felt welcome at school?

3. What are the things that your teachers do that make you feel like you are an important part of the classroom?

4. Are there times when you don't feel welcome?

5. What can we do to make this a better school, more welcoming and inclusive?

ACTION RESEARCH TOOL 7
Student Survey

What is your grade level? _____

Please select a response to each of the following questions:

	Strongly Agree	Agree	Neutral	Disagree	Strongly Disagree
Students in our school get along well.					
Students choose to interact mostly with people like themselves.					
Students in my school know how to report harassment, bullying, and racial abuse to school officials.					
Students in my school would feel comfortable reporting harassment, bullying, and racial abuse to school officials.					
Teachers in my school actively work to create a safe and welcoming environment for every student.					
Every student in my school feels like he or she belongs here.					
My school creates opportunities for students to get to know each other.					
At my school, adults and students listen to each other.					
I look forward to coming to this school in the morning.					

In the last 3 months... (please answer yes or no)

Yes   No   1. I've seen written racial vandalism or graffiti at school.

Yes   No   2. I've heard a student use a slur or derogatory put-down.

Yes   No   3. I've heard a student tease or bully another student.

Yes   No   4. I've heard a teacher or other adult in the school make disrespectful remarks about a particular group of students.

Yes   No   5. I've had a conversation with someone about our school's climate.

ACTION RESEARCH TOOL 8
Discipline Audit

Dates of Audit Review: _____ to _____

Grades Analyzed: _____

Occurrences of Suspensions and Expulsions			
	Year:	**Year:**	**Year:**
Referrals			
Suspensions			
Expulsions			

Number of Students Suspended by Ethnicity and Gender							
	African American	**Hispanic/ Latino**	**Asian/ Pacific Islander**	**Native American**	**White**	**Multiple**	**Total**
Male							
Female							
Total							

Who are the three teachers who submit the most discipline referrals?

Who are the three teachers who submit the fewest discipline referrals?

Which grade level or department has the highest rate of discipline referrals?

Which grade level or department has the lowest rate of discipline referrals?

Are there specific populations of students (e.g., English-language learners, students with disabilities, students who qualify for free lunch) who receive a disproportionate number of discipline referrals? If yes, describe.

Are there specific locations within the school that generate a disproportionate number of discipline referrals? If yes, describe.

Are there specific times during the day that a disproportionate number of discipline referrals occur? If yes, describe.

ACTION RESEARCH TOOL 9
Teacher Perspective on Problematic Student Behavior

To what extent is each of the following a problem at your school? (check those that apply and describe):

[ ] Physical conflicts among students

[ ] Robbery or theft

[ ] Gang activity

[ ] Disorder in classrooms

[ ] Disorder in hallways

[ ] Student disrespect of teachers

[ ] Threats of violence toward teachers

Choose one of the topics above and describe how it has been addressed. Has the course of action been useful? Have problems been addressed?

How much influence do teachers have over setting standards for student behavior?

When students engage in problematic behavior, are there appropriate consequences?

ACTION RESEARCH TOOL 10

Indicators of Success in Productive Group Work

INDICATORS	4—Exemplary	3—Applying	2—Approaching	1—Limited
Complexity of task: *The task is a novel application of a grade-level appropriate concept and is designed so that the outcome is not guaranteed (a chance for productive failure exists).*	Task reflects purpose and what was modeled. The task allows students an opportunity to use a variety of resources to creatively apply their knowledge of what was modeled. Students have an opportunity to experiment with concepts.	Tasks provide multiple, clear opportunities for students to apply and extend what was modeled. Students have an opportunity to use a variety of resources to creatively apply their knowledge of what was modeled.	The task is somewhat reflective of the purpose of the lesson, but there is little opportunity for student experimentation or innovation.	Task is an exact replication of what was modeled, with little or no opportunity for student experimentation with concepts.
Joint attention to tasks or materials: *Students are interacting with one another to build each other's knowledge. Outward indicators include body language and movement associated with meaningful conversations, and shared visual gaze on materials.*	Students ask critical questions of each other, developing and forming personal opinions and conclusions. They are able to evaluate and synthesize information, as well as independently use a variety of resources to acquire new or unknown information.	Body language, visual gaze, and language interactions provide evidence of joint attention to the task or materials by all members of the group. Students can explain their contributions and the contributions of other group members.	Body language, visual gaze, and language interactions provide some evidence of mutual attention to the task or materials by most members. Students are not holding each other accountable for purposeful contributions.	Students divide up the task so that they can work, then meet near end to assemble components. Body language, visual gaze, and lack of language interactions provide evidence of independent work occurring within the group.
Argumentation, not arguing: *Students use accountable talk to persuade, provide evidence, ask questions of one another, and disagree without being disagreeable.*	Students reach a better understanding or consensus based on evidence and opinions provided by others. Students hold each member of the group accountable by using questioning strategies and evidence to persuade or disagree. The conversation is respectful and courteous.	Students ask for and offer evidence to support claims. However, members continue to maintain initial beliefs or positions about a topic without considering the arguments of others. The conversation is generally respectful but some members may not participate.	There is a process in place for accountable talk. However, student dialogue is limited and there are minimal efforts to support the product. The conversation is generally respectful, but is often dominated by one member of the group or veers off-topic.	No clear process is in place to facilitate accountable talk. Lack of structure is evidence as students are off-task, in conflict, and/or are unable to complete product.

ACTION RESEARCH TOOL 10—(continued)
Indicators of Success in Productive Group Work

INDICATORS	4—Exemplary	3—Applying	2—Approaching	1—Limited
Language support: *Written, verbal, teacher, and peer supports are available to boost academic language usage.*	Sentence frames are differentiated based on students' proficiency and need. A wide range of frames are available for students and students use the frames independently in academic language and writing. Teacher modeling Includes the use of frames as well as academic vocabulary and high expectations for language production.	Students use one or two sentence frames from the variety that are available in a structured setting. A set of target vocabulary is available and used. Teachers model the use of frames. Students are encouraged to use the language support in guided instruction and productive group work.	Academic language related to the concept/standard is present. A frame may be provided. The teacher models at least once using target vocabulary or language frame. Students are encouraged to attempt using target vocabulary without opportunities for guided practice.	Vocabulary is posted but its use is not modeled. Students are simply told to use words. Language frames are not provided.
Teacher role: *What is the teacher doing while productive group work is occurring?*	Teacher is purposeful in scaffolding using prompts, cues and questions and checks for understanding regularly. Evidence collected during this time is used to plan further instruction.	Some scaffolding and checking for understanding occurs but there are delays in corrections or changes to the instruction. There is a link to further instruction.	Scaffolding or checking for understanding occurs but is not used to plan further instruction.	Teacher manages, but does not interact with groups to scaffold conceptual knowledge.
Grouping: *Small groups of 2–5 students are purposefully constructed to maximize individual strengths without magnifying areas of need (heterogeneous grouping).*	Groups are flexible and change based on students' proficiency, academic need, and/or content area. Productive group work occurs throughout the day.	Purposeful heterogeneous grouping occurs which is fluid in response to students' proficiency.	Some heterogeneous grouping occurs, but homogeneous grouping practices dominate. Decisions based on assessment are not apparent.	Grouping practices are solely homogeneous and are done primarily for scheduling convenience.

Source: Frey, N., & Fisher, D. (2010). Motivation requires a meaningful task. *English Journal, 100*(1), 30-36. Used with permission. Copyright 2010 by the National Council of Teachers of English.

ACTION RESEARCH TOOL 11
Video Analysis

Collect Examples in the Following Categories

Attributing Success to Students	Growth Mindset
Identity	Agency

ACTION RESEARCH TOOL 12
Structured Classroom Observation

Action	Targeted Student #1	Targeted Student #2	Targeted Student #3	Reflections
Equitable response opportunities				
Affirmations				
Praise				
Wait time				
Proximity				

ACTION RESEARCH TOOL 13
Learning Beliefs Survey

Please respond to the following statements according to the scale below:

1 = Strongly Agree
2 = Agree Somewhat
3 = Disagree Somewhat
4 = Strongly Disagree

_____   1. I feel that our educational system is working.

_____   2. I feel that I have the training to implement high-quality instruction successfully.

_____   3. I feel that I cover less of the curriculum because of the focus on remediation.

_____   4. I feel that I have the time to implement quality instruction effectively.

_____   5. I feel that grades are fixed and should not be changed once assigned.

_____   6. I feel that it is difficult to modify instruction and my teaching style to meet the needs of all of my students.

_____   7. I feel that allowing students multiple opportunities to demonstrate mastery is fair.

_____   8. I feel that having other adults in my classroom is a problem.

_____   9. I feel that the behaviors of some students distract the rest of a class and take away from time spent teaching.

_____   10. I feel that students take advantage of grading systems designed to be flexible.

Please complete this thought:

Learning is best accomplished when . . .

ACTION RESEARCH TOOL 14
Classroom Walkthrough/Observation

Date:	Grade:	Course:

Time:	Minutes into Class Period:	0–10 10–20 20–30
		30–40 40–50 50–60

Identify phases of gradual release evident during CWT:

    Stating/restating Content Purpose, Language Purpose, and Productive Group Work Outcome

    Modeling focus lesson or metacognitive awareness using "I" statements

    Guided instruction during PGW (question, probe, cue, direct explanation, and modeling)

    Productive group work (meaningful, interdependent collaborative group task/product)

    Independent learning

Focus on Curriculum—Purposes

What are the posted purposes for today's lesson?

Content Purpose:

Language Purpose:

PGW Outcome:

Identify the research-based components of the posted **Purposes:**

Y	N	
☐	☐	Reflect what students will learn today
☐	☐	Based on the benchmarks for the grade-level content area
☐	☐	Require students to use critical or creative thinking to:

	Acquire information	Resolve a problem	Apply a skill	Evaluate a process

☐	☐	Reflect student oral and written language needs for today's lesson
☐	☐	Show target vocabulary or academic language frames for today's lesson

Identify the type of Language **Purpose:**

	Specialized Vocabulary		Technical Vocabulary	
	Structure—grammar/ syntax	Structure—signal words	Structure—frames and templates	

ACTION RESEARCH TOOL 14—(*continued*)
Classroom Walkthrough/Observation

Identify the type of Language **Purpose:**—(*continued*)	
	Function—using language to express an opinion, summarize, persuade, question, entertain, inform, sequence, disagree, evaluate, justify, debate, describe

Focus on Instruction—Modeling and Guided Instruction

Identify observed research-based components of teacher authentic **Modeling:**

Y	N	
☐	☐	Consistently contains "I" statements (not "you" statements).
☐	☐	Focuses on teacher's expert thinking process (not directions) to apprentice students to teacher thinking.
☐	☐	Establishes relevance of the purpose beyond the classroom or for learning's sake.
☐	☐	Includes focus on text comprehension through:

	Word solving	Vocabulary	Text structure	Text features

Identify observed research-based components of teacher **Guided Instruction:**

Y	N	
☐	☐	Teacher purposefully differentiates instruction by scaffolding learning with all students.
☐	☐	Teacher responds to students' misconceptions or partial understanding with questions, cues, and prompts to guide learners in alleviating misconceptions.

Determine research-based components of teacher **Check for Understanding:**

Y	N	
☐	☐	Teacher can explain how he/she checks for understanding during and after the lesson.
☐	☐	Teacher can explain how student learning data are used to inform subsequent decisions within the current lesson and the next lesson.

Focus on the Learner—Productive Group Work and Independent Learning

Identify grouping format:

Individual	Two students	Three students	Four students	Whole class

Classroom Walkthrough/Observation

Focus on the Learner—Productive Group Work and Independent Learning—(*continued*)

Determine complexity of student work (Depth of Knowledge Level):

4: Extended thinking requiring complex thinking, reasoning, and planning, possibly relating concepts within or between content areas

3: Strategic thinking requiring reasoning, developing a plan or a sequence of steps, some complexity, more than one possible answer

2: Basic application of skills and concepts; using information or conceptual knowledge, two or more steps

1: Recall or reproduction of a fact, information, or procedure

Randomly selected students can explain in their own words:

Y	N	
☐	☐	What they are learning
☐	☐	What they are expected to produce to demonstrate learning
☐	☐	The relevance of their learning beyond the classroom or for learning's sake

Determine observed research-based components of student **Productive Group Work:**

Y	N	
☐	☐	Students are engaged in a relevant challenge, innovative task, or problem to solve that applies the concepts of the Content Purpose.
☐	☐	Students find the task challenging yet not impossible to successfully accomplish with teacher support.
☐	☐	Students have the opportunity for experimentation with concepts (not replicating what the teacher modeled).
☐	☐	Students use a variety of resources to experiment with concepts and apply their knowledge.
☐	☐	Students use critical or creative thinking to consolidate their learning and refine their skills.
☐	☐	Students actively interact with one another to build each other's knowledge. Indicators include body language, movement, language associated with meaningful conversations, and shared visual gaze on materials.
☐	☐	Student conversation is respectful and courteous, allowing them to disagree without being disagreeable.
☐	☐	Students hold each member of the group accountable by asking questions of one another.

ACTION RESEARCH TOOL 14—(*continued*)
Classroom Walkthrough/Observation

Determine observed research-based components of student **Productive Group Work:**—(*continued*)		
Y	**N**	
☐	☐	Students ask for and provide evidence to persuade or disagree, to support claims, and to reach a better understanding or consensus based on evidence and opinions provided by others.
☐	☐	Students communicate using the target vocabulary or academic sentence frames.
☐	☐	Students exhibit respect for classroom resources and equipment.

Student individual accountability (structured interaction) within the PGW is evidenced through:	
Defined group-dependent roles	Collaborative written task that identifies each member's contribution (e.g., colors)
Collaborative data sheet/template/chart	Individual data sheet for group lab/task
Purposeful discussion (pair-share, round robin)	Other:

Determine observed research-based components of **Independent Learning:**		
Y	**N**	
☐	☐	Students apply what they have learned to novel tasks that they understand and can successfully complete.
☐	☐	Student novel tasks help refine their skills and build their expertise.

Focus on Classroom Learning Environment		
Y	**N**	
☐	☐	Posted models/exemplars of quality student work show expectations of Purposes.
☐	☐	Scoring guides or rubrics are clearly posted in student-friendly language.
☐	☐	Evident routines and procedures for a safe and orderly environment show students take appropriate ownership and responsibility for learning.

Note: Created by Page Dettmann

ACTION RESEARCH TOOL 15
Homework Audit

Teacher: _____   Grade level: _____

Date: _____   Content focus: _____

Completion Analysis

Number of Students Assigned Homework Task: _____

Number of Students Who Completed the Task Correctly: _____

Number of Students Who Completed the Task Incorrectly: _____

Number of Students Who Did Not Complete the Task: _____

% Correct completers: _____   % Negative practice: _____

Task Analysis

Purpose of Homework	Characteristics	Evidence
Fluency Building	Multiple opportunities for practice Focuses on one or two skills Serves as an access point for other skills or knowledge	
Application	Allows a skill to be used to solve a problem, or apply a rule or principle Uses previously learned skill for a new situation	
Spiral Review	Student utilizes previously learned skills or knowledge Allows student to confirm his or her understanding and assess his or her own learning Related conceptually to current learning	
Extension	Potential for development of new understandings Results in a new product or innovation Requires the use of a variety of skills or knowledge	

ACTION RESEARCH TOOL 15—(*continued*)
Homework Audit

Reflective Analysis

Do students fully understand how the skill is performed?

Is the difficulty level low enough so that they can focus on speed/rate/fluency, instead of how it is performed?

What rule or principle will the students use to solve the problem?

Do the students possess the background knowledge and prior experiences necessary to understand the new or novel situation?

What previously taught skills or knowledge are important for future learning and assessment?

In what ways will this strengthen students' metacognitive awareness of how well they use skills and knowledge?

What previously taught skills or knowledge serve as a basis for current classroom instruction?

Does the assignment lead to a new knowledge base or set of concepts?

Will the students create a new product or innovation that they have not done before?

What skills or knowledge will students require to complete the assignment?

ACTION RESEARCH TOOL 16
Grit Scale

Directions for taking the Grit Scale: Please respond to the following 17 items. Be honest—there are no right or wrong answers!

1. I aim to be the best in the world at what I do.
   - ☐ Very much like me
   - ☐ Mostly like me
   - ☐ Somewhat like me
   - ☐ Not much like me
   - ☐ Not like me at all

2. I have overcome setbacks to conquer an important challenge.
   - ☐ Very much like me
   - ☐ Mostly like me
   - ☐ Somewhat like me
   - ☐ Not much like me
   - ☐ Not like me at all

3. New ideas and projects sometimes distract me from previous ones.
   - ☐ Very much like me
   - ☐ Mostly like me
   - ☐ Somewhat like me
   - ☐ Not much like me
   - ☐ Not like me at all

4. I am ambitious.
   - ☐ Very much like me
   - ☐ Mostly like me
   - ☐ Somewhat like me
   - ☐ Not much like me
   - ☐ Not like me at all

5. My interests change from year to year.
   - ☐ Very much like me
   - ☐ Mostly like me
   - ☐ Somewhat like me
   - ☐ Not much like me
   - ☐ Not like me at all

6. Setbacks don't discourage me.
   - ☐ Very much like me
   - ☐ Mostly like me
   - ☐ Somewhat like me
   - ☐ Not much like me
   - ☐ Not like me at all

ACTION RESEARCH TOOL 16—(*continued*)
Grit Scale

7. I have been obsessed with a certain idea or project for a short time but later lost interest.
   - ☐ Very much like me
   - ☐ Mostly like me
   - ☐ Somewhat like me
   - ☐ Not much like me
   - ☐ Not like me at all

8. I am a hard worker.
   - ☐ Very much like me
   - ☐ Mostly like me
   - ☐ Somewhat like me
   - ☐ Not much like me
   - ☐ Not like me at all

9. I often set a goal but later choose to pursue a different one.
   - ☐ Very much like me
   - ☐ Mostly like me
   - ☐ Somewhat like me
   - ☐ Not much like me
   - ☐ Not like me at all

10. I have difficulty maintaining my focus on projects that take more than a few months to complete.
    - ☐ Very much like me
    - ☐ Mostly like me
    - ☐ Somewhat like me
    - ☐ Not much like me
    - ☐ Not like me at all

11. I finish whatever I begin.
    - ☐ Very much like me
    - ☐ Mostly like me
    - ☐ Somewhat like me
    - ☐ Not much like me
    - ☐ Not like me at all

12. Achieving something of lasting importance is the highest goal in life.
    - ☐ Very much like me
    - ☐ Mostly like me
    - ☐ Somewhat like me
    - ☐ Not much like me
    - ☐ Not like me at all

ACTION RESEARCH TOOL 16—(*continued*)
Grit Scale

13. I think achievement is overrated.
- ☐ Very much like me
- ☐ Mostly like me
- ☐ Somewhat like me
- ☐ Not much like me
- ☐ Not like me at all

14. I have achieved a goal that took years of work.
- ☐ Very much like me
- ☐ Mostly like me
- ☐ Somewhat like me
- ☐ Not much like me
- ☐ Not like me at all

15. I am driven to succeed.
- ☐ Very much like me
- ☐ Mostly like me
- ☐ Somewhat like me
- ☐ Not much like me
- ☐ Not like me at all

16. I become interested in new pursuits every few months.
- ☐ Very much like me
- ☐ Mostly like me
- ☐ Somewhat like me
- ☐ Not much like me
- ☐ Not like me at all

17. I am diligent.
- ☐ Very much like me
- ☐ Mostly like me
- ☐ Somewhat like me
- ☐ Not much like me
- ☐ Not like me at all

Directions for scoring the Grit Scale

For questions 1, 2, 4, 6, 8, 11, 12, 14, 15, and 17, assign the following points:

5 = Very much like me

4 = Mostly like me

3 = Somewhat like me

2 = Not much like me

1 = Not like me at all

ACTION RESEARCH TOOL 16—(*continued*)
Grit Scale

For questions 3, 5, 7, 9, 10, 13, and 16, assign the following points:

- 1 = Very much like me
- 2 = Mostly like me
- 3 = Somewhat like me
- 4 = Not much like me
- 5 = Not like me at all

Grit is calculated as the average score for items 2, 3, 5, 6, 7, 8, 9, 10, 11, 14, 16, and 17. The Consistency of Interest subscale is calculated as the average score for items 3, 5, 7, 9, 10, and 16. The Perseverance of Effort subscale is calculated as the average score for items 2, 6, 8, 11, 14, and 17.

The Brief Grit Scale score is calculated as the average score for items 3, 6, 7, 8, 9, 10, 11, and 17.

Ambition is calculated as the average score for items 1, 4, 12, 13, and 15.

Grit Scale Citations

Duckworth, A. L, & Quinn, P. D. (2009). Development and validation of the Short Grit Scale (Grit-S). *Journal of Personality Assessment, 91*, 166–174. http://www.sas.upenn.edu/~duckwort/images/Duckworth%20and%20Quinn.pdf

Duckworth, A. L., Peterson, C., Matthews, M. D., & Kelly, D. R. (2007). Grit: Perseverance and passion for long-term goals. *Journal of Personality and Social Psychology, 9*, 1087–1101.

ACTION RESEARCH TOOL 17
Academic Recovery Audit

Percentage of Students on Academic Recovery Plan by Grade or Subject:

Greatest need area:

Least need area:

Based on an analysis of the Academic Recovery Contract:

What areas cause students to struggle?

What strategies are commonly being recommended?

How effective have previous contracts been?

ACTION RESEARCH TOOL 18

Teachers' Sense of Efficacy Scale

Teachers' Sense of Efficacy Scale[1] (long form)

Teacher Beliefs	How much can you do?								
Directions: This questionnaire is designed to help us gain a better understanding of the kinds of things that create difficulties for teachers in their school activities. Please indicate your opinion about each of the statements below. Your answers are confidential.	Nothing	Very Little		Some Influence		Quite A Bit		A Great Deal	
1. How much can you do to get through to the most difficult students?	(1)	(2)	(3)	(4)	(5)	(6)	(7)	(8)	(9)
2. How much can you do to help your students think critically?	(1)	(2)	(3)	(4)	(5)	(6)	(7)	(8)	(9)
3. How much can you do to control disruptive behavior in the classroom?	(1)	(2)	(3)	(4)	(5)	(6)	(7)	(8)	(9)
4. How much can you do to motivate students who show low interest in school work?	(1)	(2)	(3)	(4)	(5)	(6)	(7)	(8)	(9)
5. To what extent can you make your expectations about student behavior clear?	(1)	(2)	(3)	(4)	(5)	(6)	(7)	(8)	(9)
6. How much can you do to get students to believe they can do well in school work?	(1)	(2)	(3)	(4)	(5)	(6)	(7)	(8)	(9)
7. How well can you respond to difficult questions from your students ?	(1)	(2)	(3)	(4)	(5)	(6)	(7)	(8)	(9)
8. How well can you establish routines to keep activities running smoothly?	(1)	(2)	(3)	(4)	(5)	(6)	(7)	(8)	(9)
9. How much can you do to help your students value learning?	(1)	(2)	(3)	(4)	(5)	(6)	(7)	(8)	(9)
10. How much can you gauge student comprehension of what you have taught?	(1)	(2)	(3)	(4)	(5)	(6)	(7)	(8)	(9)
11. To what extent can you craft good questions for your students?	(1)	(2)	(3)	(4)	(5)	(6)	(7)	(8)	(9)
12. How much can you do to foster student creativity?	(1)	(2)	(3)	(4)	(5)	(6)	(7)	(8)	(9)
13. How much can you do to get children to follow classroom rules?	(1)	(2)	(3)	(4)	(5)	(6)	(7)	(8)	(9)

[1]Because this instrument was developed at the Ohio State University, it is sometimes referred to as the *Ohio State Teacher Efficacy Scale*. We prefer the name *Teachers' Sense of Efficacy Scale*.

ACTION RESEARCH TOOL 18—(*continued*)
Teachers' Sense of Efficacy Scale

Teachers' Sense of Efficacy Scale (long form)—(*continued*)

Teacher Beliefs	Nothing	Very Little	Some Influence	Quite A Bit	A Great Deal
Directions: This questionnaire is designed to help us gain a better understanding of the kinds of things that create difficulties for teachers in their school activities. Please indicate your opinion about each of the statements below. Your answers are confidential.			**How much can you do?**		
14. How much can you do to improve the understanding of a student who is failing?	(1) (2)	(3) (4)	(5) (6)	(7) (8)	(9)
15. How much can you do to calm a student who is disruptive or noisy?	(1) (2)	(3) (4)	(5) (6)	(7) (8)	(9)
16. How well can you establish a classroom management system with each group of students?	(1) (2)	(3) (4)	(5) (6)	(7) (8)	(9)
17. How much can you do to adjust your lessons to the proper level for individual students?	(1) (2)	(3) (4)	(5) (6)	(7) (8)	(9)
18. How much can you use a variety of assessment strategies?	(1) (2)	(3) (4)	(5) (6)	(7) (8)	(9)
19. How well can you keep a few problem students from ruining an entire lesson?	(1) (2)	(3) (4)	(5) (6)	(7) (8)	(9)
20. To what extent can you provide an alternative explanation or example when students are confused?	(1) (2)	(3) (4)	(5) (6)	(7) (8)	(9)
21. How well can you respond to defiant students?	(1) (2)	(3) (4)	(5) (6)	(7) (8)	(9)
22. How much can you assist families in helping their children do well in school?	(1) (2)	(3) (4)	(5) (6)	(7) (8)	(9)
23. How well can you implement alternative strategies in your classroom?	(1) (2)	(3) (4)	(5) (6)	(7) (8)	(9)
24. How well can you provide appropriate challenges for very capable students?	(1) (2)	(3) (4)	(5) (6)	(7) (8)	(9)

ACTION RESEARCH TOOL 18—(*continued*)
Teachers' Sense of Efficacy Scale

Teachers' Sense of Efficacy Scale (short form)

Teacher Beliefs	How much can you do?								
Directions: This questionnaire is designed to help us gain a better understanding of the kinds of things that create difficulties for teachers in their school activities. Please indicate your opinion about each of the statements below. Your answers are confidential.	Nothing		Very Little		Some Influence		Quite A Bit		A Great Deal
1. How much can you do to control disruptive behavior in the classroom?	(1)	(2)	(3)	(4)	(5)	(6)	(7)	(8)	(9)
2. How much can you do to motivate students who show low interest in school work?	(1)	(2)	(3)	(4)	(5)	(6)	(7)	(8)	(9)
3. How much can you do to get students to believe they can do well in school work?	(1)	(2)	(3)	(4)	(5)	(6)	(7)	(8)	(9)
4. How much can you do to help your students value learning?	(1)	(2)	(3)	(4)	(5)	(6)	(7)	(8)	(9)
5. To what extent can you craft good questions for your students?	(1)	(2)	(3)	(4)	(5)	(6)	(7)	(8)	(9)
6. How much can you do to get children to follow classroom rules?	(1)	(2)	(3)	(4)	(5)	(6)	(7)	(8)	(9)
7. How much can you do to calm a student who is disruptive or noisy?	(1)	(2)	(3)	(4)	(5)	(6)	(7)	(8)	(9)
8. How well can you establish a classroom management system with each group of students?	(1)	(2)	(3)	(4)	(5)	(6)	(7)	(8)	(9)
9. How much can you use a variety of assessment strategies?	(1)	(2)	(3)	(4)	(5)	(6)	(7)	(8)	(9)
10. To what extent can you provide an alternative explanation or example when students are confused?	(1)	(2)	(3)	(4)	(5)	(6)	(7)	(8)	(9)
11. How much can you assist families in helping their children do well in school?	(1)	(2)	(3)	(4)	(5)	(6)	(7)	(8)	(9)
12. How well can you implement alternative strategies in your classroom?	(1)	(2)	(3)	(4)	(5)	(6)	(7)	(8)	(9)

ACTION RESEARCH TOOL 18—(*continued*)
Teachers' Sense of Efficacy Scale

Directions for Scoring the Teachers' Sense of Efficacy Scale

Developers: Megan Tschannen-Moran, College of William and Mary
Anita Woolfolk Hoy, the Ohio State University

Construct Validity

For information on the construct validity of the Teachers' Sense of Teacher efficacy Scale, see Tschannen-Moran, M., & Woolfolk Hoy, A. (2001). Teacher efficacy: Capturing and elusive construct. *Teaching and Teacher Education, 17,* 783–805.

Factor Analysis

It is important to conduct a factor analysis to determine how your participants respond to the questions. We have consistently found three moderately correlated factors—*Efficacy in Student Engagement, Efficacy in Instructional Practices,* and *Efficacy in Classroom Management*—but at times the makeup of the scales varies slightly. With preservice teachers we recommend that the full 24-item scale (or 12-item short form) be used, because the factor structure often is less distinct for these respondents.

Subscale Scores

To determine the *Efficacy in Student Engagement, Efficacy in Instructional Practices,* and *Efficacy in Classroom Management* subscale scores, we compute unweighted means of the items that load on each factor. Generally these groupings are as follows:

Long Form

Efficacy in Student Engagement:	Items	1, 2, 4, 6, 9, 12, 14, 22
Efficacy in Instructional Strategies:	Items	7, 10, 11, 17, 18, 20, 23, 24
Efficacy in Classroom Management:	Items	3, 5, 8, 13, 15, 16, 19, 21

Short Form

Efficacy in Student Engagement:	Items	2, 3, 4, 11
Efficacy in Instructional Strategies:	Items	5, 9, 10, 12
Efficacy in Classroom Management:	Items	1, 6, 7, 8

Reliabilities

In Tschannen-Moran, M., & Woolfolk Hoy, A. (2001). Teacher efficacy: Capturing and elusive construct. *Teaching and Teacher Education, 17,* 783–805, the following were found:

	Long Form			Short Form		
	Mean	SD	alpha	Mean	SD	alpha
OSTES	7.1	.94	.94	7.1	.98	.90
Engagement	7.3	1.1	.87	7.2	1.2	.81
Instruction	7.3	1.1	.91	7.3	1.2	.86
Management	6.7	1.1	.90	6.7	1.2	.86

ACTION RESEARCH TOOL 19
School Improvement Action Plan

Name	
School	

Analyze the Data

Describe findings from the analysis of student achievement data.	
List questions that your analysis raised.	
Identify priority needs based on this analysis.	

Clarify the Problem

Collect additional quantitative and qualitative data that provide a context for the data you analyzed.	
Identify root causes and contributing factors that might explain the existing data.	
Identify the target group you have selected for your plan and justify.	

Create Your Action Research Plan

Identify annual goals and objectives for your plan.	
Describe how you will involve leadership, teachers, families, and students in this plan.	

ACTION RESEARCH TOOL 19—(*continued*)
School Improvement Action Plan

Create Your Action Research Plan—(*continued*)

Identify what evidence you will accept as obtainment of the objectives.	
Based on your problem clarification findings, describe the interventions and systems you will implement to address your problem.	
Describe the progress-monitoring data you will collect to determine progress toward the objectives.	
Identify professional development needed to implement the plan.	

Implement and Monitor Your Action Plan

Map out a calendar of activities for the year.	
Create a timeline for data collection and analysis.	
Develop a plan for communicating progress and results to stakeholders.	
Analyze progress-monitoring results.	
Identify needed revisions to the plan based on progress-monitoring data.	
Communicate progress on any needed changes.	

References

Abel, D. C. (Ed.). (1992). *Theories of human nature: Classical and contemporary readings.* New York: McGraw-Hill.

Alloway, M. (2010). Facing your reflection. *Principal Leadership, 10*(9), 82–84.

Bandura, A. (1986). *Social foundations of thought and action: A social cognitive theory.* Englewood Cliffs, NJ: Prentice-Hall.

Bandura, A. (1996). *Self-efficacy: The exercise of control.* New York: Freeman.

Bandura, A. (2001). Social cognitive theory: An agentic perspective. *Annual Review of Psychology, 56,* 1–26.

Berman, P., McLaughlin, M., Bass, G., Pauly, E., & Zellman, G. (1977). *Federal programs supporting educational change: Vol VII. Factors affecting implementation and continuation.* (Report No. R-1589/7-HEW). Santa Monica, CA: RAND. (ERIC Document Reproduction Service No. 140432)

Blankstein, A. M. (2004). *Failure is not an option: Six principles that guide student achievement in high-performing schools.* Thousand Oaks, CA: Corwin.

Block, P. (2008). *Community: The structure of belonging.* San Francisco: Berrett-Koehler.

Borko, H. (2004). Professional development and teacher learning: Mapping the terrain. *Educational Researcher, 33*(8), 3–15.

Boudett, K. P., City, E., & Murnane, R. J. (2005). *Data wise: A step-by-step guide to using assessment results to improve teaching and learning.* Cambridge, MA: Harvard University Press.

Bransford, J. D., Brown, A. L., & Cocking, R. R. (Eds.). (2000). *How people learn: Brain, mind, experience, and school.* Committee on Developments in the Science of Learning and Committee on Learning Research and Educational Practice, Commission on Behavioral and Social Sciences and Education, National Research Council. Washington, DC: National Academies Press.

Calhoun, E. (1999). *How to use action research in the self-renewing school*. Alexandria, VA: ASCD.

Canady, R. L., & Retting, M. D. (1995). *Block scheduling: A catalyst for change in high schools*. Princeton, NJ: Eye on Education.

Canfield, J. (2007). *Chicken soup for the soul in the classroom*. Deerfield Beach, FL: HCI.

Cazden, C. B. (2001). *Classroom discourse: The language of teaching and learning*. Portsmouth, NH: Heinemann.

Chenoweth, K. (2010). Leaving nothing to chance. *Educational Leadership, 68*(3), 16–21.

City, E. A., Elmore, R. F., Fiarman, S. E., & Tietel, L. (2009). *Instructional rounds in education: A network approach to improving teaching and learning*. Cambridge, MA: Harvard Educational Press.

Coleman-Kiner, A. (June 8, 2011). Leading with love. *Education Week, 30*(33), 25.

Collins, J. C., & Porras, J. I. (1998). Building your company's vision. In Harvard Business Review *on change* (pp. 21–54). Boston: Harvard Business School Press.

Costello, B., Wachtel, J., & Wachtel, T. (2009). *Restorative practices handbook for teachers, disciplinarians and administrators*. Bethlehem, PA: International Institute for Restorative Practices.

Covey, S. R. (2004). *The 7 habits of highly effective people* (Rev. ed.). New York: Free Press.

Csikszentmihalyi, M. (1990). *Flow: The psychology of optimal experience*. New York: Harper & Row.

Deal, T. E., & Peterson, K. D. (1999). *Shaping school culture: The heart of leadership*. San Francisco: Jossey-Bass.

Deal, T. E., &. Peterson, K. D. (2009). *Shaping school culture: Pitfalls, paradoxes, & promises* (2nd ed.). San Francisco: Jossey-Bass.

Deming, W. E. (1986). *Out of the crisis*. Cambridge, MA: Massachusetts Institute of Technology.

Denton, P. (2007). *The power of our words: Teacher language that helps children learn*. Turners Falls, MA: Northeast Foundation for Children.

DiJulius, J. R., III. (2003). *Secret service: Hidden systems that deliver unforgettable customer service*. New York: AMACOM.

DiJulius, J. R., III. (2008). *What's the secret? To providing a world-class customer experience*. New York: Wiley.

Duckworth, A. L., Peterson, C., Matthews, M. D., & Kelly, D. R. (2007). Grit: Perseverance and passion for long-term goals. *Journal of Personality and Social Psychology, 92*(6), 1087–1101.

Duckworth, A. L, & Quinn, P. D. (2009). Development and validation of the Short Grit Scale (Grit-S). *Journal of Personality Assessment, 91*, 166–174. http://www.sas.upenn.edu/~duckwort/images/Duckworth%20and%20Quinn.pdf

DuFour, R. (2004). Schools as learning communities. *Educational Leadership, 61*(8), 6–11.

Dweck, C. S. (2006). *Mindset: The new psychology of success*. New York: Ballantine.

Education Trust. (2011). *Dispelling the myth: Ware Elementary Kansas.* Retrieved from http://www.edtrust.org/dc/publication/ware-elementary

Erikson, E. (1968). *Identity, youth and crisis.* New York: Norton.

Fisher, D., Everlove, S., & Frey, N. (2009). Not just another literacy meeting. *Principal Leadership, 9*(9), 40–43.

Fisher, D., & Frey, N. (2006). Majority rules: A schoolwide literacy success. *Principal Leadership, 6*(7), 16–20.

Fisher, D., & Frey, N. (2008a). *Better learning through structured teaching: A framework for the gradual release of responsibility.* Alexandria, VA: ASCD.

Fisher, D., & Frey, N. (2008b). Homework and the gradual release of responsibility: Making responsibility possible. *English Journal, 98*(2), 40–45.

Fisher, D., & Frey, N. (2010). *Enhancing RTI: How to ensure success with effective classroom instruction and intervention.* Alexandria, VA: ASCD.

Fisher, D., & Frey, N. (2011). *The purposeful classroom: How to structure lessons with learning goals in mind.* Alexandria, VA: ASCD.

Fisher, D., & Frey, N. (2012). *Improving adolescent literacy: Content area strategies at work* (3rd ed.). Boston: Allyn & Bacon.

Fisher, D., Frey, N., & Grant, M. (2009). A diploma that matters: Schoolwide efforts to improve high school teaching and learning. In S. R. Parris, D. Fisher, & K. Headley (Eds.), *Adolescent literacy, field-tested: Effective solutions for every classroom* (pp. 191–203). Newark, DE: International Reading Association.

Fisher, D., Frey, N., & Lapp, D. (2011). Focusing on the participation and engagement gap: A case study on closing the achievement gap. *Journal of Education for Students Placed at Risk, 16,* 56–64.

Fisher, D., & Kennedy, C. (2001). *Inclusive middle schools.* Baltimore, MD: Brookes.

Fisher, D., Sax, C., & Pumpian, I. (1999). *Inclusive high schools.* Baltimore: Brookes.

Florian, D. (1997). *In the swim.* San Diego, CA: Harcourt Brace.

Frey, N. (2010). *The effective teacher's guide: 50 strategies to engage students and promote interactive learning (2nd ed.).* New York: Guilford.

Frey, N., & Fisher, D. (2011). *The formative assessment action plan: Practical steps to more successful teaching and learning.* Alexandria, VA: ASCD.

Frey, N., Fisher, D., & Nelson, J. (2010). Lessons from the melting pot. *Journal of Staff Development, 31*(5), 24–28.

Fullan, M. (2001). *Leading in a culture of change.* San Francisco: Jossey-Bass.

Fullan, M. (2008). *The six secrets of change: What the best leaders do to help their organizations survive and thrive.* San Francisco: Jossey-Bass.

Fullan, M., & St. Germain, C. (2006). *Learning places: A field guide for improving the context of schooling.* Thousand Oaks, CA: Corwin.

Galton, F. (1886). Regression towards mediocrity in hereditary stature. *Journal of the Anthropological Institute of Great Britain and Ireland, 15,* 246–226.

Gill, M. G., & Hoffman, B. (2009). Shared planning time: A novel context for studying teachers' discourse and beliefs about learning and instruction. *Teachers College Record, 111*(5), 1242–1273.

Gladwell, M. (2005). *Blink: The power of thinking without thinking.* New York: Little, Brown.

Gloger, S. (1971). An improved grading system. *Education, 92*(1), 95.

Goetsch, D. L., & Davis, S. B. (2010). *Quality management for organizational excellence: Introduction to total quality* (6th ed.). Upper Saddle River, NJ: Pearson.

Goodman, J. F. (2011, May 25). When students are silenced. *Education Week, 30*(32), 20, 22.

Grandau, L. (2005). Learning from self-study: Gaining knowledge about how fourth graders move from relational description to algebraic generalization. *Harvard Educational Review, 75*(2), 202–221.

Guskey, T. R. (2000). *Evaluating professional development.* Thousand Oaks, CA: Corwin.

Guskey, T. R. (2008). *Practical solutions for serious problems in standards-based grading.* Thousand Oaks, CA: Corwin.

Hattie, J. (2009). *Visible learning: A synthesis of over 800 meta-analyses relating to achievement.* New York: Routledge.

Hill, J. D., & Flynn, K. M. (2006). *Classroom instruction that works with English language learners.* Alexandria, VA: ASCD.

Hoy, W. K., Tarter, C. J., & Kottkamp, R. B. (1991). *Open schools/healthy schools: Measuring organizational climate.* Newbury Park, CA: Sage.

Hunter, M. C. (1976). *Improved instruction.* Thousand Oaks, CA: Corwin.

Jerald, C. D. (2006). *School culture: "The hidden curriculum."* Washington, DC: Center for Comprehensive School Reform and Improvement. Retrieved from www.centerforcsri.org.

Johnston, P. H. (2004). *Choices words: How our language affects children's learning.* Portland, ME: Stenhouse.

Jordi, R. (2011). Refraining the concept of reflection: Consciousness, experiential learning, and reflective learning practices. *Adult Education Quarterly, 61*, 181–197.

Jorgensen, C. M., McSheehan, M., & Sonnenmeier, R. M. (2007). Presumed competence reflected in the educational programs of students with IDD before and after the Beyond Access professional development intervention. *Journal of Intellectual & Developmental Disability, 32*, 248–262.

Joyce, B. R., & Showers, B. (2002). *Student achievement through staff development* (3rd ed.). Alexandria, VA: ASCD.

Juran, J. M. (1970). *Quality planning and analysis.* New York: Macmillan.

Kapur, M. (2008). Productive failure. *Cognition and Instruction, 26*, 379–424.

Katz, L., Sax, C., & Fisher, D. (2003). *Activities for a diverse classroom: Connecting students* (2nd ed.). Colorado Springs, CO: PEAK Parent Center.

Kennedy, C. H., & Fisher, D. (2001). *Inclusive middle schools.* Baltimore: Brookes.

Kohlberg, L. (1981). *Essays on moral development, Vol. I: The philosophy of moral development.* San Francisco: Harper & Row.

Kohn, A. (1999). *Punished by rewards: The trouble with gold stars, incentive plans, A's, praise, and other bribes.* Boston: Houghton Mifflin.

Kunc, N. (2000). Rediscovering the right to belong. In R. A. Villa & J. Thousand (Eds.), *Restructuring for caring and effective education: Piecing the puzzle together* (2nd ed., pp. 77–92). Baltimore: Brookes.

Langer, G. M., Colton, A. B., & Goff, L. S. (2003). *Collaborative analysis of student work: Improving teaching and learning.* Alexandria, VA: ASCD.

Lareau, A. (2003). *Unequal childhoods: Class, race, and family life.* Los Angeles: University of California Press.

Leading and Managing at Work. (2005). *Who is Dr. W. Edwards Deming?* Retrieved from www.lii.net/deming.html

Lee, V. E., & Smith, J. B. (1999). Social support and achievement for young adolescents in Chicago: The role of school academic press. *American Educational Research Journal, 36,* 907–945.

Lorden, D. H. (2010). Effects of professional development intervention on middle school principals to increase their knowledge of and ability to increase teacher efficacy. (Unpublished doctoral dissertation). San Diego State University, San Diego, CA.

Louden, R. B. (2010). *The world we want: How and why the ideals of the Enlightenment still elude us.* New York: Oxford University Press.

Lujan, N., & Day, B. (2010). Professional learning communities: Overcoming the roadblocks. *Delta Kappa Gamma Bulletin, 76*(2), 10–17.

Lunden, S. C., Paul, H., & Christensen, J. (2000). *Fish! A remarkable way to boost morale and improve results.* New York: Hyperion.

Maguad, B. A. (1999). *A total quality approach to Adventist teaching.* Retrieved from http://www.aiias.edu/ict/vol_24/24cc_157-176.htm.

Markow, D., Kim, A., & Liebman, M. (2007). *The MetLife survey of the American teacher: The homework experience.* New York: Metropolitan Life Insurance Company. Retrieved June 26, 2011, from http://www.eric.ed.gov/ERICDocs/data/ericdocs2sql/content_storage_01/0000019b/80/3c/f3/74.pdf.

Maslow, A. H. (1943). A theory of human motivation. *Psychological Review, 50*(4), 370–396.

Maxwell, G., & Liu, J. (Eds.). (2007). *Restorative justice and practices in New Zealand: Toward a restorative society.* Wellington, New Zealand: School of Government, Victoria University of Wellington.

Maxwell, J. C. (2008). *Leadership gold: Lessons I've learned from a lifetime of leading.* Nashville, TN: Thomas Nelson.

Medina, J. (2008). *Brain rules: 12 principles for surviving and thriving at work, home and school.* Seattle, WA: Pear Press.

Moses, R. P. (2001). Algebra and activism: Removing the shackles of low expectations. A conversation with Robert P. Moses. *Educational Leadership, 59*(2), 6–11.

O'Connor, K. (2009). *How to grade for learning K–12* (3rd ed.). Thousand Oaks, CA: Corwin.

Pearson, P. D., & Gallagher, G. (1983). The gradual release of responsibility model of instruction. *Contemporary Educational Psychology, 8*, 112–123.

Peña, C., & León, L. (2011). The use of digital video to foster reflective practice in teacher education. *International Journal of Instructional Media, 38*(2), 125–132.

Pine, B. J., & Gilmore, J. H. (2011). *The experience economy.* Boston: Harvard Business School Press.

Popham, W. J. (2010). *Classroom assessment: What teachers need to know* (6th ed.). Boston: Allyn & Bacon.

Reeves, D. (2011). *Elements of grading.* Bloomington, IN: Solution Tree.

Reynolds, L. (2010). New Jersey high school does away with D's. *Curriculum Review, 50*(2), 8.

Riessman, C. K. (1993). *Narrative analysis.* Newbury Park, CA: Sage.

Robinson, K., & Aronica, L. (2009). *The element: How finding your passion changes everything.* New York: Viking.

Ryan, P. M. (1999). *Riding freedom.* New York: Scholastic.

Samuels, M. L. (1991). Statistical reversion toward the mean: More universal than regression toward the mean. *The American Statistician, 45*, 344–346.

Sapon-Shevin, M. (1998). *Because we can change the world: A practical guide to building cooperative, inclusive classroom communities.* Boston: Allyn & Bacon.

Sax, C., & Fisher, D. (2001). Using qualitative action research to effect change: Teachers becoming reflective practitioners. *Teacher Education Quarterly, 28*(2), 71–80.

Schmoker, M. (2006). *Results now: How we can achieve unprecedented improvements in teaching and learning.* Alexandria, VA: ASCD.

Schultz, H., & Yang, D. J. (1999). *Pour your heart into it: How Starbucks built a company one cup at a time.* New York: Hyperion.

Sharp HealthCare. (2007). *Malcolm Baldrige National Quality Award Application: Health care category.* San Diego, CA: Author. Retrieved from www.quality.nist.gov/PDF_files/2007_Sharp_Application_Summary.pdf

Snyder, D. (2011). Preparing for Teaching through Reflection. *Music Educators Journal, 97*(3), 56–60.

Steinberg, M. P., Allensworth, E., & Johnson, D. W. (2011). *Student and teacher safety in Chicago Public Schools: The roles of community context and school social organization.* Chicago: Consortium on Chicago School Research at the University of Chicago.

Stringer, E. T. (2007). *Action research* (3rd ed.). Thousand Oaks, CA: Sage.

Studer Group. (2005). *The magic of rounding.* Retrieved from http://www.studergroup.com/dotCMS/knowledgeAssetDetail?inode=111088

Studer, Q. (2003). *Hardwiring excellence: Purpose, worthwhile work, making a difference.* Gulf Breeze, FL: Fire Starter Publishing.

Thomas, R. S. (2011, June 15). My nine "truths" of data analysis. *Education Week, 36*, 29.

Townsend, B. L. (2000). The disproportionate discipline of African American learners: Reducing school suspensions and expulsions *Exceptional Children, 66*, 381–391.

Tracy, K. (2002). *Everyday talk: Building and reflecting identities.* New York: Guilford.

Tschannen-Moran, M. & Barr, M. (2004). Fostering student achievement: The relationship between collective teacher efficacy and student achievement. *Leadership and Policy in Schools, 3*, 187–207.

Tschannen-Moran, M., & Hoy, A. (2007). The differential antecedents of self-efficacy beliefs of novice and experienced teachers. *Teaching and Teacher Education, 23*(6), 944–956.

Tschannen-Moran, M., & Woolfolk Hoy, A. (2001). Teacher efficacy: Capturing and elusive construct. *Teaching and Teacher Education, 17*, 783–805.

Villa, R. A., & Thousand, J. (Eds.). (2000). *Restructuring for caring and effective education: Piecing the puzzle together* (2nd). Baltimore: Paul Brookes.

Webster-Wright, A. (2009). Reframing professional development through understanding authentic professional learning. *Review of Educational Research, 79*(2), 702–739.

Wheatley, M. J. (1998). *A simpler way*. San Francisco: Berrett-Koehler.

White, S. H. (2011). *Show me the proof! Tools and strategies to make data work with the common core state standards*. Englewood, CO: Lead+Learn Press.

Wiggins, G., & McTighe, J. (2005). *Understanding by design* (Expanded 2nd ed.). Alexandria, VA: ASCD.

Williams, T., Haertel, E., & Kirst, M. W. (2011). *Improving middle grades math performance: A closer look at district and school policies and practices, course placements, and student outcomes in California*. Mountain View, CA: EdSource.

Zander, R., & Zander, B. (2002). *The art of possibility: Transforming professional and personal life*. New York, Penguin.

Index

In this index the Action Research Tools are found in title case. The letter *f* following a page number denotes a figure.

About the Authors

Douglas Fisher, PhD, is a professor of educational leadership at San Diego State University and a teacher leader at Health Sciences High & Middle College. He is a member of the California Reading Hall of Fame and is the recipient of a Celebrate Literacy Award from the International Reading Association, the Farmer Award for Excellence in Writing from the National Council of Teachers of English, and a Christa McAuliffe Award for Excellence in Teacher Education from the American Association of State Colleges and Universities. He has published numerous articles on improving student achievement, and his books include *The Purposeful Classroom, Enhancing RTI: How to Ensure Success with Effective Classroom Instruction and Intervention, Checking for Understanding,* and *Content-Area Conversations.* He can be reached at dfisher@mail.sdsu.edu.

Nancy Frey, PhD, is a professor of literacy in the School of Teacher Education at San Diego State University and a teacher leader at Health Sciences High & Middle College. Before joining the university faculty, Nancy was a special education teacher in the Broward County (Florida) Public Schools, where she taught students at the elementary and middle school levels. She later worked for the Florida Department of Education on a statewide project for supporting students with disabilities in a general education curriculum. Nancy is a recipient of the Christa McAuliffe Award for Excellence in Teacher

Education from the American Association of State Colleges and Universities and the Early Career Award from the National Reading Conference. Her research interests include reading and literacy, assessment, intervention, and curriculum design. She has published many articles and books on literacy and instruction, including *Productive Group Work* and *Better Learning Through Structured Teaching*. She can be reached at nfrey@mail.sdsu.edu.

Ian Pumpian, PhD, is a Professor in the Department of Educational Leadership at San Diego State University with a Ph.D. from the University of Wisconsin. He has taught, supervised, and chaired dissertations of several San Diego lead principals and area superintendents. He cofounded Health Science High and Middle College and currently serves as the CEO/President. Previously Dr. Pumpian served as the Executive Director of the City Heights Educational Collaborative where he assumed superintendent-level responsibilities over the educational programs of these 5000 students, professional development for their 300+ teachers, and a comprehensive professional development school that annually involved over 125,000 hours of SDSU faculty and student credential and advanced degree teaching, research, and practica activities. Dr. Pumpian has authored and co-authored numerous journal articles and books. He can be reached at ipumpian@mail.sdsu.edu.

Related ASCD Resources: School Culture

At the time of publication, the following ASCD resources were available (ASCD stock numbers appear in parentheses). For up-to-date information about ASCD resources, go to www.ascd.org. You can search the complete archives of *Educational Leadership* at http://www.ascd.org/el.

Multimedia

Creating the Capacity for Change: An ASCD Action Tool by Jody Mason Westbrook and Valarie Spisder-Albert (#702118)

Making School Improvement Happen with What Works in Schools: An ASCD Action Tool Set (Three Tools) by John L. Brown (#705055)

Schooling by Design: An ASCD Action Tool (#707039)

Networks

Visit the ASCD web site (www.ascd.org) and click on About ASCD. Go to the section on Networks for information about professional educators who have formed groups around topics such as "Restructuring Schools." Look in the Network Directory for current facilitators' addresses and phone numbers.

Online Courses

Visit the ASCD web site (www.ascd.org) for the following professional development opportunities:

Leadership for Contemporary Schools by Vera Blake (#PD09OC07)

Schools as Professional Learning Communities: An Introduction by Vera Blake and Diane Jackson (#PD09OC28)

What Works in Schools: An Introduction by John Brown (#PD09OC13)

Print Products

Accountability for Learning: How Teachers and School Leaders Can Take Charge by Douglas B. Reeves (#104004)

Align the Design: A Blueprint for School Improvement by Nancy J. Mooney and Ann T. Mausbach (#108005)

Connecting Leadership with Learning: A Framework for Reflection, Planning, and Action by Michael Copland and Michael Knapp (#105003)

Creating the Opportunity to Learn: Moving from Research to Practice to Close the Achievement Gap by Wade Boykin and Pedro Noguera (#107016)

Enhancing Student Achievement: A Framework for School Improvement by Charlotte Danielson (#102109)

How to Help Your School Thrive Without Breaking the Bank by John G. Gabriel and Paul C. Farmer (#107042)

The Learning Leader: How to Focus School Improvement for Better Results by Douglas B. Reeves (#105151)

The Results Fieldbook: Practical Strategies from Dramatically Improved Schools by Mike Schmoker (#101001)

Turning High-Poverty Schools into High-Performing Schools by William H. Parrett and Kathleen Budge (#109003)

Videos and DVDs

What Works in Schools (DVD and Facilitator's Guide) (#603047)

Leadership Strategies for Principals (DVD and *The New Principal's Fieldbook: Strategies for Success* by Pam Robbins and Harvey Alvy) (#608033)

The Results Video Series (DVD and Online Facilitator's Guide) (#601261)

A Visit to a Data-Driven School District (DVD and Viewer's Guide) (#606059)

WHOLE CHILD The Whole Child Initiative helps schools and communities create learning environments that allow students to be healthy, safe, engaged, supported, and challenged. To learn more about other books and resources that relate to the whole child, visit www.wholechildeducation.org.

For more information: send e-mail to member@ascd.org; call 1-800-933-2723 or 703-578-9600, press 2; send a fax to 703-575-5400; or write to Information Services, ASCD, 1703 N. Beauregard St., Alexandria, VA 22311-1714 USA.